KINGFISHER

First published 2008 by Kingfisher
an imprint of Macmillan Children's Books
a division of Macmillan Publishers Limited
20 New Wharf Road, London N1 9RR
Basingstoke and Oxford
www.panmacmillan.com

Associated companies throughout the world

ISBN 978-0-7534-1589-4

Copyright © Macmillan Children's Books 2008

9 8 7 6 5 4 3 2 1
1TR/1107/WKT/PICA/140MA/C

A CIP catalogue record for this book is available from the British Library.

Printed in China

Contents

How this book works   6

DINOSAURS   7

Early dinosaurs   8
Meat-eaters   10
Tyrannosaurus rex   12
Plant-eaters   14
Brachiosaurus   16
Ancient sea reptiles   18
Flying reptiles   20
Early mammals   22
Record breakers   24

LAND ANIMALS 25

Elephants	26
Lions	28
Tigers	30
Wolves	32
Flightless birds	34
Bears	36
Pandas	38
Polar bears	40
Jungle animals	42
Apes and monkeys	44
Bugs and beetles	46
Ants	48
Butterflies and moths	50
Farm animals	52
Dogs	54
Cats	56
Record breakers	58

SEA CREATURES 59

Blue whales	60
Dolphins	62
Killer whales	64
Seals	66
Sharks	68
Wading birds	70
Penguins	72
Albatrosses	74
Record breakers	76

PEOPLE AND PLACES 77

Savannahs	78
Grasslands	80
Jungles	82
Mountains	84
Volcanoes	86
Earthquakes	88
Villages	90
Cities	92
On the farm	94
On the beach	96
At home	98
At school	100
Bronze Age	102
Ancient Egypt	104
Mummies	106
Buried treasure	108
Record breakers	110

TRANSPORT 111

Cars	112
Racing cars	114
Trucks	116
Diggers	118
Trains	120
Ships	122
Aeroplanes	124
Rockets	126
Record breakers	128

Answers 129

Dinosaurs	130
Land animals	134
Sea creatures	142
People and places	146
Transport	154
Record breakers	156

Index 158

How this book works

Read all about it first! Start with the introduction and follow the boxes across the pages from left to right and top to bottom. Look at the pictures, too, because sometimes the answers can be found there. Then it is time to tackle the questions...

1. Eight questions

The questions are on the far left. In addition to general questions, there are true or false options and sometimes you have to unjumble letters to find the answer!

2. Follow the numbers!

All the answers are somewhere on the page. If you do not know the answer straight away, each question has a matching number in an orange or blue circle to help you find the right place to start reading.

3. Find the answer

When you have answered all the questions, turn to the back of the book to see if you were right!

Chapter one
DINOSAURS

Early dinosaurs   8
Meat-eaters   10
Tyrannosaurus rex   12
Plant-eaters   14
Brachiosaurus   16
Ancient sea reptiles   18
Flying reptiles   20
Early mammals   22
Record breakers   24

Early dinosaurs

The dinosaurs were a large group of reptiles. The first dinosaur lived about 245 million years ago. The last ones died out 65 million years ago.

1 What does 'dinosaur' mean?

2 All dinosaurs were small. True or false?

3 How many types of dinosaur were there?

4 Did dinosaurs lay eggs?

5 Unjumble DOOPRSAU to spell a type of dinosaur.

6 What were meat-eating dinosaurs called?

7 Did crocodiles live at the same time as the dinosaurs?

8 How did a *Coelophysis* move?

Terrible name 1 2 3
The word dinosaur means 'terrible lizard'. There were probably about 10,000 types of dinosaur. Many of them were much larger than any reptiles living today.

Ancient life 4 5 6 7

Dinosaurs laid eggs and had scaly skin. There were two main types of dinosaur: theropods were meat-eaters and had clawed feet. Sauropods were giant plant-eaters. Other reptiles, such as crocodiles and lizards, lived at the same time.

pterosaur (flying reptile)

sauropod

theropod

crocodile

lizard

Coelophysis

long jaw

Two feet 8

One of the earliest hunting dinosaurs was *Coelophysis*. It ran on its back legs and snapped up small reptiles in its toothy jaws.

Meat-eaters

Dinosaurs are among the largest and fiercest hunters that have ever lived. Some of them would have towered above elephants and giraffes!

1 Where did the *Allosaurus* live?

2 What did the *Allosaurus* use to kill prey?

3 When did the *Albertosaurus* live?

4 How did the *Albertosaurus* kill its victims?

5 *Deinonychus* moved slowly. True or false?

6 Did *Deinonychus* ever hunt in groups?

7 What does '*Deinonychus*' mean?

8 Unjumble the word WALC.

Dagger teeth   1 2

The *Allosaurus* was a huge hunter that lived in North America about 150 million years ago. It killed prey with its jagged teeth.

Allosaurus

Neck crusher 3 4

Albertosaurus hunted about 70 million years ago. It chased prey by running on its back legs. It killed its victim with a bite to the back of the neck.

Albertosaurus

Deinonychus

Runner 5 6

Deinonychus was a fast-running hunter from America. It killed giant plant-eaters, perhaps working in groups like wolves do today.

Hooked claws 7 8

The name *Deinonychus* means 'terrible claw'. The hunter's largest claw was on its second toe and was used to slash prey.

Tyrannosaurus rex

The most famous dinosaur of all, *Tyrannosaurus rex*, was as tall as a house and had teeth that were as long as your foot! It was a very skilled hunter.

1 *Tyrannosaurus rex* ate dead bodies. True or false?

2 How did *T. rex* find dead bodies?

3 Did *T. rex* stand on four legs?

4 Was *T. rex* fast?

5 Re-arrange GGEDAJ ETEHT to name something used by *T. rex* when hunting.

6 What does 'Tyrannosaurus rex' mean?

7 When did *T. rex* live?

8 Where have most *T. rex* fossils been discovered?

Flesh feast 1 2

Tyrannosaurus rex (*T.rex*) scavenged for food, sniffing out the bodies of animals that had died naturally, and then eating them!

Weapons   3 4 5

T. rex stood on two legs. It could not run very fast and attacked prey by surprise. It used its long, jagged teeth and the claws on its feet to rip flesh off a body. The tiny arms were not used in hunting.

Lizard king   6 7 8

The name *Tyrannosaurus rex* means 'king of the tyrant lizards' – a tyrant is a cruel ruler. *T. rex* lived about 70 million years ago. Its teeth were the size of bananas! Most *T. rex* fossils have been found in North America.

Plant-eaters

The largest types of dinosaur ate plants. They chewed leaves and branches, and they swallowed stones to grind up the food inside their stomachs!

1 The *Apatosaurus* was bigger than a blue whale. True or false?

2 What is another name for the *Apatosaurus*?

3 Unjumble SUROTUESGAS.

4 What were the plates on a *Stegosaurus* for?

5 What was on a *Stegosaurus*'s tail?

6 What does '*Triceratops*' mean?

7 What are the horns of a *Triceratops* for?

8 What protects a *Triceratops*'s neck?

Monster leaf-eater 1 2
The *Apatosaurus* was one of the largest dinosaurs ever. It was almost as large as today's blue whale. The *Apatosaurus* is also known as the *Brontosaurus*.

Apatosaurus

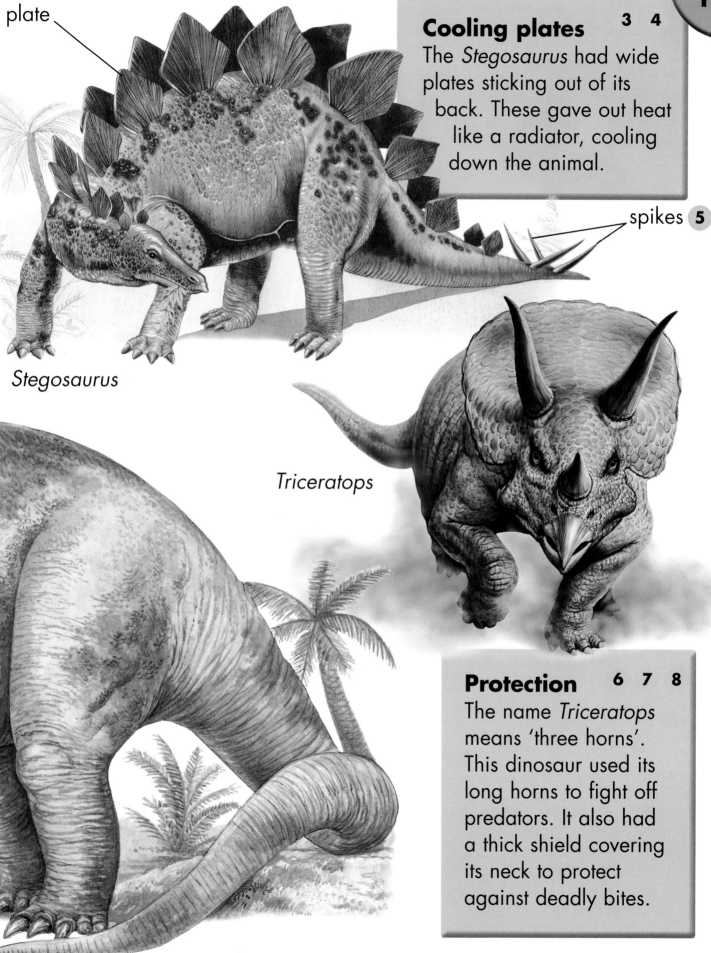

plate

Cooling plates 3 4
The *Stegosaurus* had wide plates sticking out of its back. These gave out heat like a radiator, cooling down the animal.

spikes 5

Stegosaurus

Triceratops

Protection 6 7 8
The name *Triceratops* means 'three horns'. This dinosaur used its long horns to fight off predators. It also had a thick shield covering its neck to protect against deadly bites.

Brachiosaurus

The *Brachiosaurus* lived about 140 million years ago. Like a giraffe it had long legs and a long neck for reaching leaves high in the trees.

1 Unjumble ELAESV to spell food eaten by a *Brachiosaurus*.

2 What made their teeth blunt?

3 Where were its nostrils?

4 Nostrils may have helped their sense of smell. True or false?

5 What else may the nostrils have been used for?

6 How heavy was a *Brachiosaurus*?

7 Which is taller, a *Brachiosaurus* or a telephone pole?

8 How long was a *Brachiosaurus*?

Crushing jaw   1   2

Brachiosaurus was a plant-eater with many teeth, which it used to crush leaves and woody branches. This tough food often made their teeth blunt.

Head holes 3 4 5

Brachiosaurus had nostrils on a ridge on top of its head. These might have given the dinosaur a powerful sense of smell, or they could have been used to make loud calls.

nostril

Size up 6 7

The *Brachiosaurus* weighed 77 tonnes – the same as ten double-decker buses! It was a very long dinosaur, and it was taller than a telephone pole.

teeth

8

← 22 metres long →

Ancient sea reptiles

While dinosaurs ruled the land, other types of reptile ruled the ocean. Most of these sea creatures are extinct. Only turtles have survived.

1 When did the *Archelon* live?

2 What did *Archelon* eat?

3 How long was an *Archelon*?

4 Which sea reptile looked like a dolphin?

5 Plesiosaurs had long necks. True or false?

6 What did a *Placodus* eat?

7 What did *Globidens* crush?

8 Unjumble SAUROTHON to spell an ocean reptile with sharp teeth.

Giant shell 1 2 3
Archelon was an early turtle that lived 220 million years ago. It was as long as a car and ate shellfish.

Archelon

Placodus

plesiosaur

flipper

Crunching shells 6 7
Many ocean reptiles ate
shellfish. The *Placodus* and
Globidens used flat teeth
to crush shells. They
ate the soft bits
and spat out
the rest.

Body shape 4 5
Water reptiles were like
today's sea creatures.
Ichthyosaurs looked
like dolphins, while
plesiosaurs were more
like long-necked seals.

Globidens

8 nothosaur

ichthyosaur

Flying reptiles

The pterosaurs were relatives of the dinosaurs. Although they looked similar to birds, pterosaurs had no feathers and were not early types of bird.

1 What does 'pterosaur' mean?

2 Was a pterosaur's wing made of skin?

3 The wing contained a long finger. True or false?

4 Were pterosaurs very good at flying?

5 How did cliff-living pterosaurs catch their food?

6 Was *Dimorphodon* a fast runner?

7 Unjumble TCSNIE to spell food eaten by *Dimorphodon*.

8 Was the largest flying animal a pterosaur?

Finger wing　　1　2　3
The word pterosaur means 'winged lizard'. The wing was made of skin that stretched out behind a super-long finger.

Pteranodon

Dimorphodon

Cliff jumpers   4 5

Pterosaurs were not great flyers. They found it difficult to get into the air. Some jumped off sea cliffs to do so. They swooped over the water, scooping up fish. Then they rode warm, rising air before gliding back to their perches.

Little snapper   6 7

The *Dimorphodon* could fly, but it was also a fast runner. It snapped up flying insects with its large jaws and it also caught small animals on the ground.

Largest ever!   8

Many pterosaurs were sparrow-sized, but the largest pterosaur was the biggest animal ever to fly. Each wing was as long as a football goal.

Early mammals

Mammals are not related to dinosaurs. Instead, they come from an even older type of reptile. The first mammals lived about 100 million years ago.

1 Re-arrange SPARUMILAS.

2 Where are marsupial babies kept after birth?

3 Where do most marsupials live today?

4 Mammals lived at the same time as dinosaurs. True or false?

5 What happened when dinosaurs became extinct?

6 Did mammals eat dinosaur eggs?

7 Dinosaurs had hair. True or false?

8 Does a mammal's hair keep it warm?

Pocket baby   1   2   3

Many early mammals were marsupials. Marsupials give birth to tiny babies, which then continue to grow inside a pouch on their mother's belly. Today, marsupials are rare. Most of them live in Australia.

baby in pouch

Tyrannosaur

Survivors 4 5

Small mammals lived alongside dinosaurs. They were often preyed on by the hunters. When the dinosaurs died out, mammals took over.

Egg feasts 6

As dinosaur eggs were full of protein and nutrients, they were good food. Some early mammals may have been big enough to break into the eggs to eat them!

Hairy coats 7 8

Unlike dinosaurs, mammals have hair on their bodies. The hairs keep the animals warm. Mammals can survive in much colder weather than dinosaurs.

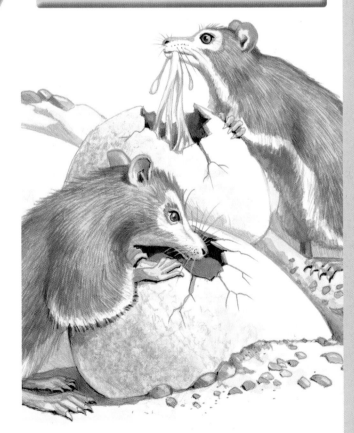

DINOSAURS
Record breakers

1. The dinosaurs became extinct after a 10-kilometre-wide meteor hit Mexico 65 million years ago.

2. The first dinosaur fossil was identified in 1841.

3. When the dinosaurs roamed the Earth, the continents were connected together to make a huge area of land called Pangaea.

4. The largest meat-eating dinosaur was *Spinosaurus*. It was 21 metres long.

5. The biggest dinosaur ever discovered is *Amphicoelias*. It weighed 122 tonnes.

6. Biologists know that dinosaurs did not all die out. Some evolved into the birds we see today.

7. The most ancient types of reptile are the turtles and tortoises. They evolved 280 million years ago.

8. The smallest dinosaurs were about the size of a chicken.

9. The largest dinosaur bone ever found is 1.5 metres long and weighed 1 tonne.

10. The cleverest dinosaur was *Troodon*. It had the largest brain compared to its body size.

Chapter two
LAND ANIMALS

Elephants 26
Lions 28
Tigers 30
Wolves 32
Flightless birds 34
Bears 36
Pandas 38
Polar bears 40
Jungle animals 42
Apes and monkeys 44
Bugs and beetles 46
Ants 48
Butterflies and moths 50
Farm animals 52
Dogs 54
Cats 56
Record breakers 58

Elephants

The African elephant is the biggest land animal. Asian elephants are slightly smaller. Elephants are endangered. They are hunted for their tusks.

1 What is a group of elephants called?

2 Are male elephants in charge of the herd?

3 What is an elephant's tusk made of?

4 Can you train an elephant to work?

5 Unjumble NALABINH to spell a famous general's name.

6 Do elephants eat leaves and grass?

7 Elephants eat for 16 hours a day. True or false?

8 Are plants a high-energy food?

Hannibal's army

All in the family **1** **2**

Elephants live in big groups called herds. Female elephants are in charge of life in an elephant family. Elephant babies drink their mother's milk.

At war **4** **5**

Young elephants are smart and easy to train. They have worked with people for thousands of years. In 218 BCE, Hannibal, a great general, took elephants across the snowy Alps to fight the Romans.

Hungry **6** **7** **8**

An elephant reaches up into a tree to pull down leaves. Elephants eat grass, too. Plants are not a high-energy food so elephants must eat lots of them. They eat for 16 hours a day.

Lions

The lion is a powerful type of cat. Nearly all lions live in Africa, on grassland called savannah. The lions hunt large animals, such as zebras. They kill with a bite to the neck.

1 What is the thick hair on a lion's neck called?

2 Male and female lions are the same size. True or false?

3 What is a group of lions called?

4 Who rules a group of lions?

5 What are baby lions called?

6 Which member of the pride always eats first?

7 Unjumble SENOSIL to work out who raises a baby lion.

8 What does a male lion do if he meets another male?

King of beasts 1 2

A male lion has a thick mane of hair on his neck. Male lions are larger, heavier and stronger than the females.

Family 3 4 5 6

Lions live in groups called prides. Prides are ruled by a single male. The other members are lionesses (females) and cubs (baby lions). Lionesses do the hunting, but the male gets to eat first!

Keeping control 7 8

Lionesses work together to raise their cubs. The male does little to help. Instead, he spends his time fighting off rival males, who come to take over the pride.

rival male

Tigers

1 Why do tigers have stripes?

2 Do tigers make much noise when they walk?

3 Unjumble RIGESTS to give the word for a female tiger.

4 How long does a tiger cub stay with its mother?

5 Tigers live in large groups. True or false?

6 How do tigers keep their claws sharp?

7 How does a tiger get close to prey?

8 How do tigers kill their prey?

The tiger is the world's largest cat. It lives in the jungles of Asia. Tigers hunt deer and other wild animals, such as boar. They attack people only if they cannot find anything else to eat.

Sneak attack 1 2

Tigers are best known for their stripes. Dark stripes on orange fur help the tiger stay hidden among the shadows. A tiger can walk almost silently on its soft, wide feet.

Growing up ③ ④

A tigress (female tiger) gives birth to about six cubs every three years. Only one or two of the cubs survive. They live with their mother for two years and learn how to hunt.

Living alone ⑤ ⑥

Tigers live alone. They scratch long marks into tree trunks. This keeps their claws razor sharp, and the scratches also warn other tigers to stay away.

In for the kill ⑦ ⑧

A tiger hides in the undergrowth and creeps up on its prey. It then charges out of its hiding place and smashes into the victim, knocking it over. The tiger breaks the prey's neck swiftly with its mighty jaws.

alking

charging

the catch!

Wolves

The wolf is the largest wild dog in the world. It is the ancestor of all breeds of pet dog. Wolves live in groups called packs. Most wolves live in the forests of Canada and Siberia.

1 Which small animal might a wolf catch?

2 When do wolves hunt as a team?

3 Unjumble NURNGIN to give something wolves are very good at.

4 How far can a wolf run in a day?

5 A group of wolves is called a flock. True or false?

6 How many pack members have cubs each year?

7 Why do wolves howl?

8 How far away can you hear a wolf howling?

Hunting team 1 2
In summer, wolves hunt by themselves for hares, which are similar to rabbits, and other small animals. In winter, the wolf pack works as a team to kill bigger animals, such as deer.

Star runner 3 4

A wolf's body is built for running long distances. It has big lungs and a strong heart so it does not get tired quickly. A wolf can run 200 kilometres in a day.

Pair up 5 6

A wolf pack is organized according to strict rules. Only one male and female in the pack has cubs, but the other wolves in the pack help to look after the young.

Midnight howler 7 8

People once thought wolves howled at the moon. In fact, they are telling other wolves where they are and warning them to stay away! A howl can be heard up to 16 kilometres away.

Flightless birds

Not all birds can fly. In fact, the world's largest birds are too heavy to leave the ground. Their wings are very small, and they have long legs used for running fast.

1 Cassowaries live in the desert. True or false?

2 Unjumble SQAECU to name the bone on a cassowary's head.

3 What is the cassowary's casque used for?

4 What is the largest bird in the world?

5 Where do ostriches live?

6 How does an ostrich escape from danger?

7 How did the emu get its name?

8 How does an emu find fresh food?

Bone head ① ② ③

The cassowary lives in the forests of New Guinea in Asia. It has a bone spike on its head, called a casque. The bird pushes branches out of the way with its casque.

casque

cassowary

emu

Giant runner **4 5 6**

The ostrich is the world's largest bird – it can grow to 2.75 metres tall. Ostriches live in Africa. They keep out of danger by running away. Ostriches can reach speeds of 70 kilometres per hour.

ostrich

Rain bird **7 8**

The largest bird in Australia is the emu. It gets its name from the call it makes. Emus eat shoots and flowers that sprout after rain. The birds follow rain clouds to find fresh food.

Bears

Bears are the world's biggest land predators. A predator is an animal that hunts other animals for food. Most bears live in the forests of North America and Asia.

1 How do bears climb trees?

2 How long are the claws of a brown bear?

3 Unjumble EVEEBIH for the place where bears find honey.

4 Bears never eat fish. True or false?

5 Where do bears often gather to catch fish?

6 Bears can catch fish with their teeth. True or false?

7 Do bears like to eat nuts and berries?

8 How do bears eat honey?

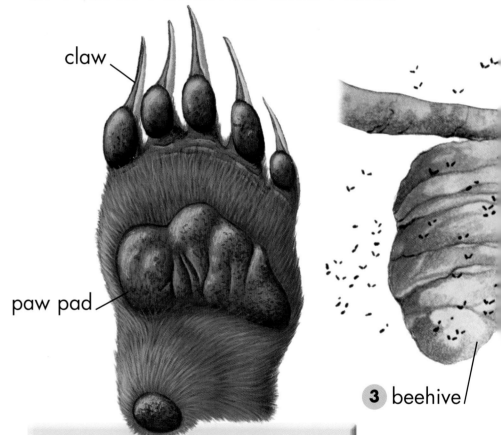

claw

paw pad

3 beehive

Slash and grab **1** **2**
Bears have long claws for slashing prey, digging dens and gripping bark when climbing trees. Brown bears have the biggest claws. They are 10 centimetres long.

Catching fish ④ ⑤ ⑥

Bears like to catch salmon and trout from rivers. The bears gather around waterfalls where these fish are easy to find. They knock the prey out of the water with their huge paws or catch them with their sharp teeth.

Yummy! ⑦ ⑧

Bears also like to eat nuts and berries. They love honey, too. Small bears climb trees and rip open beehives. They lick the honey out with their tongues and they even eat the bees!

Pandas

The giant panda is a type of bear. It eats bamboo, which provides little energy. Pandas must eat a lot to stay alive. They can sleep for only four hours before waking up hungry again!

1 Why do pandas have white faces with black eyes and ears?

2 Re-arrange OBAMOB for the plant pandas eat.

3 Where do pandas sleep?

4 What sticks out of a panda's wrist?

5 How long does it take for a panda cub to grow up?

6 Which country do pandas live in?

7 How many pandas live in the wild?

8 Do pandas live on mountains?

Black eyes 1

Pandas are known for their black-and-white fur. The black eyes and ears make it easier to see each other in the forest.

bamboo 2

Living in the forest 3 4 5

Pandas do not have a den –
they sleep in the open. They hold
bamboo using a sixth 'finger',
which sticks out from each wrist.
Pandas have cubs every two
years. A cub takes about
four years to grow up.

Wild ones 6 7 8

Pandas are very rare.
They live only in
China, where about
1,000 wild pandas
live in small patches
of bamboo forest
on mountainsides.

Polar bears

The polar bear is the world's largest bear. The males are as large as a family-size car. For most of the year, polar bears hunt for food on the frozen seas that surround the North Pole.

1 Is a polar bear's hair white?

2 Why do bears store a layer of fat under the skin?

3 Unjumble END to name the place cubs are born.

4 How long do cubs stay in the den?

5 What does a polar bear mother eat when she is in the den with her cubs?

6 What do polar bears hunt?

7 Where do they wait for prey?

8 Polar bears catch seals with fishing rods. True or false?

Life on ice ① ②

A polar bear's fur looks white, but the hairs are actually see-through. Each bear has a layer of fat under its skin, so it can survive if it cannot find food.

Snow mother 3 4 5

Polar bears give birth in winter inside a den under the snow. The cubs stay there for three months, living on their mother's milk. The mother will not eat at all until she and the cubs leave in spring.

large paw

Fierce hunter 6 7 8

Polar bears hunt seals by lying in wait for them beside holes in the ice. Then the bears kill them with a blow of a paw.

Jungle animals

Many interesting and different animals live in jungles. Jungles grow where it is very hot and wet all year round. That is why jungles are sometimes called rainforests.

1 Why are jungles being cut down?

2 Why are some jungle animals rare?

3 Unjumble VAJNA to spell the name of a rare rhino.

4 How many horns does a Javan rhino have?

5 How do toucans crack nuts?

6 How long is a quetzal's tail?

7 What would happen if someone touched the red frog?

8 Where does the ocelot hunt?

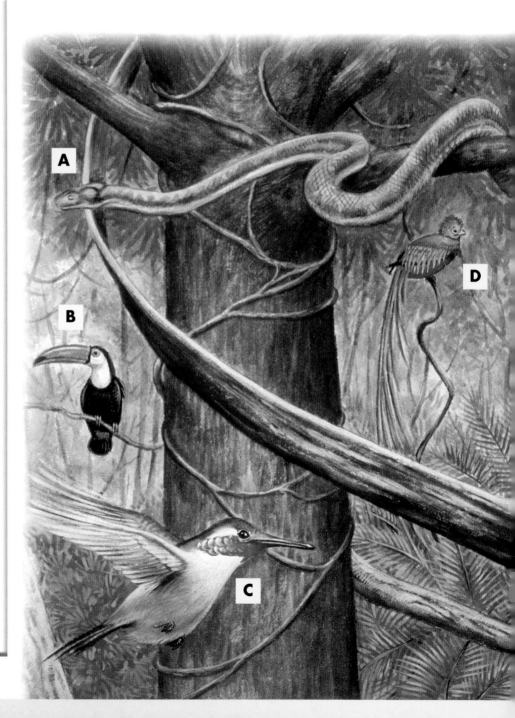

Rare creatures 1 2 3 4

Large areas of jungle are being cut down to make room for farms. Jungle animals are now rare because they have few places to live. One of the rarest of all is the Javan rhino (left). Unlike most other rhinos, this type has just one horn.

Amazon 5 6 7 8

These animals live in South America's Amazon rainforest:

A Tree snake

B Toucan. It cracks nuts with its big beak.

C Hummingbird

D Quetzal. Its tail is four times longer than the rest of its body.

E Howler monkey

F Sloth. It hangs upside down.

G Vampire bat

H Frog. Its skin is deadly to the touch.

I Ocelot. It hunts in the undergrowth.

Apes and monkeys

People often get confused between monkeys and apes, but they are different in many ways. Monkeys are small and have tails, while apes are big and have no tails.

1 Where could you find a wild gorilla?

2 Which ape lives in southeast Asia?

3 What is the most common type of ape in the world?

4 When do howler monkeys call?

5 How far away can a howler monkey's call be heard?

6 Where is a howler monkey's voicebox?

7 Unjumble DRIMLALN to spell the name of the largest monkey.

8 Where do mandrills live?

Rare relatives   ① ② ③

Apes include the gorillas and chimpanzees of Africa, and orang-utans from southeast Asia. All these animals are very rare. The only common ape is the human – you and me!

orang-utan

Wake up! ④ ⑤ ⑥

Howler monkeys bellow loudly in the morning. The calls can be heard three kilometres away. Their call is so loud because of the large voicebox in their bulging throats.

Funny face ⑦ ⑧

The mandrill is the biggest monkey in the world. It lives deep in the jungles of Africa. Male mandrills have colourful faces and sharp fangs to frighten their enemies.

Bugs and beetles

There are half a million types of bug and beetle! Bugs suck their food, while beetles bite theirs. Ladybirds and weevils are common beetles, while cicadas and pondskaters are types of bug.

1 What do bugs have instead of bones?

2 How do bugs breathe?

3 A water bug has hairy legs to keep warm. True or false?

4 How do water bugs catch fish?

5 What do stag beetles use their pincers for?

6 Unjumble NATENANE for insect feelers.

7 How many legs does a bug have?

8 Where do beetles keep their wings?

Outer skin ① ②

A bug does not have bones. Instead, it has a hard skin, which gives the body its shape. The bug breathes air through holes in its skin.

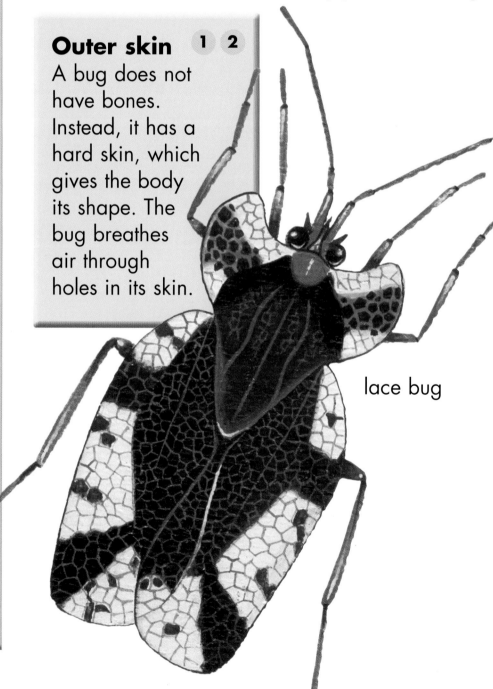

lace bug

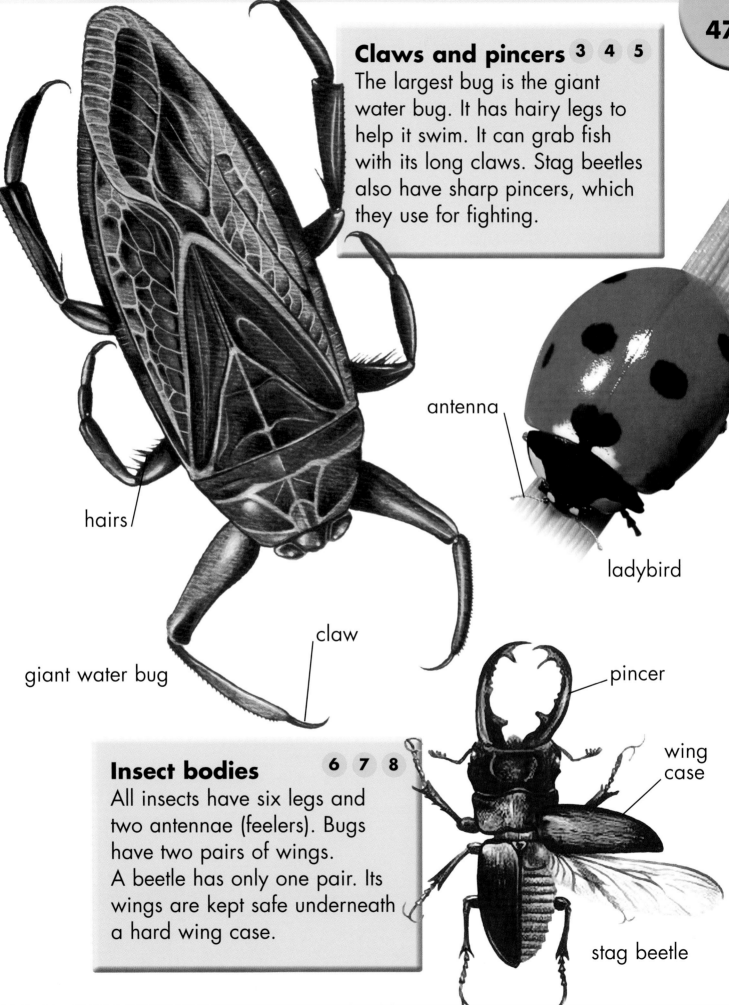

Claws and pincers ③ ④ ⑤

The largest bug is the giant water bug. It has hairy legs to help it swim. It can grab fish with its long claws. Stag beetles also have sharp pincers, which they use for fighting.

antenna

ladybird

hairs

claw

giant water bug

pincer

wing case

Insect bodies ⑥ ⑦ ⑧

All insects have six legs and two antennae (feelers). Bugs have two pairs of wings. A beetle has only one pair. Its wings are kept safe underneath a hard wing case.

stag beetle

Ants

Thousands of ants live together inside nests. Each nest has one queen ant, and only she may lay eggs. Most of the eggs hatch into female ants, which spend their lives working for the queen.

1 Where do weaver ants live?

2 Baby ants are called larvae. True or false?

3 What do larvae make to glue leaves together?

4 Which ants defend the nest?

5 Soldier ants are armed with sharp jaws, and what other weapon?

6 Where might you find an ant nest?

7 Which type of ant gathers food?

8 Unjumble UPAPE to find the name for ant cocoons.

Leaf nests
1 2 3

Weaver ants build a nest of leaves for the queen and her young. The ants hold the leaves together and grip larvae (baby ants) in their jaws. The larvae make sticky silk that glues the leaves together.

adult ant holds larva

Defence force ④ ⑤

Most nests have a force of fierce soldier ants to keep the queen safe. They have sharp jaws for biting and stingers in their tails.

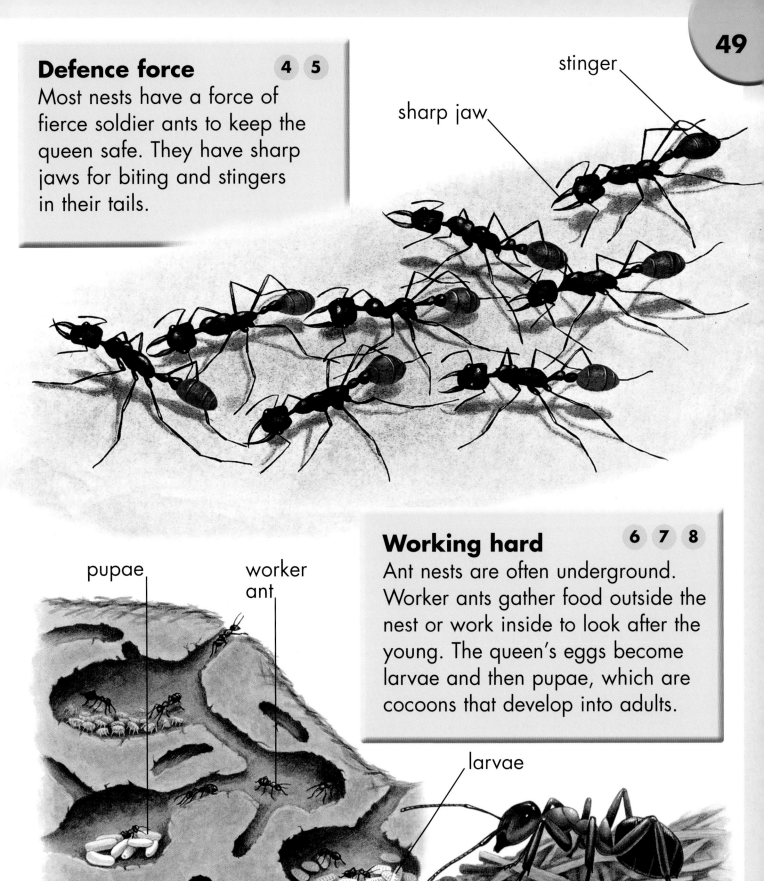

stinger

sharp jaw

pupae

worker ant

larvae

Working hard ⑥ ⑦ ⑧

Ant nests are often underground. Worker ants gather food outside the nest or work inside to look after the young. The queen's eggs become larvae and then pupae, which are cocoons that develop into adults.

Butterflies and moths

Large and colourful, butterflies are very delicate insects. They are seen most often in the summer, fluttering around flowers in parks and gardens.

1 What hatches from a butterfly egg?

2 What do caterpillars eat?

3 What is the name of the silk bag that a caterpillar spins?

4 Unjumble CRAMNOH to spell the name of a common butterfly.

5 Moths fly at night. True or false?

6 Which are more colourful, moths or butterflies?

7 How many wings do butterflies have?

8 What is the mouthpart of a butterfly called?

Stages of life   1 2 3

A butterfly egg hatches into a caterpillar. It eats leaves and fruit, then spins a silk bag (cocoon) around itself. Once inside, the caterpillar grows wings and changes into a butterfly. The butterfly emerges from the cocoon.

monarch **4**

caterpillar

red admiral

Colourful wings 5 6

Moths are similar to butterflies, but they fly at night instead. They are dull in colour so they can hide in the dark. Butterflies come out in the day, so their wings are brightly patterned.

Camberwell beauty

eggs

peacock butterfly

Flying insects 7 8

Butterflies have four wings (two pairs). The front wing is hooked to the back wing so they work like a single big wing. Butterflies eat only liquids. They suck their food through a long, tube-shaped mouthpart called a proboscis.

Farm animals

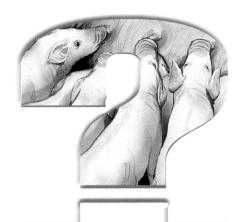

The animals on farms provide us with milk, eggs and, of course, meat. The animals produce other things, too. Their skins become leather, and their fat is used in lotions and skin creams.

1 Cockerels lay eggs. True or false?

2 What is a female chicken called?

3 Where does wool come from?

4 Which breed of cattle is best for producing milk?

5 Unjumble FROHEERD to spell the name of a cattle breed.

6 What is special about Highland cattle?

7 Ham, pork and what other meat comes from a pig?

8 What is a female pig called?

hen   cockerel

Chickens ① ②
Eggs are laid by female chickens, or hens. A male chicken is called a cockerel. Cockerels are larger than hens and have more colourful feathers.

sheep

Curls and chops 3
Sheep are raised for their meat, called lamb or mutton, and their coats. Their curly hair is used to make wool.

Jersey

Breeds 4 5 6
Each breed or type of cattle is kept for a special reason. Jersey cows produce creamy milk, and Herefords are raised for their meat. Highland cattle have long, thick hair to keep warm in winter.

Hereford

Highland

New life 7 8
Pigs are raised for their meat, which is sold as bacon, pork and ham. Each year, a sow (female pig) gives birth to several piglets. These are killed for their meat at six months of age.

Dogs

Dogs make good pets because they are friendly, loyal and soon become part of the family. All types of dog are relatives of wolves.

1 What does 'carnivore' mean?

2 What does a dog use its teeth for?

3 Dogs have no sense of smell. True or false?

4 How many puppies can a bitch produce?

5 How long do puppies take to become adults?

6 When did dogs start to live with people?

7 What is a mongrel?

8 Unjumble GOBDULL to spell a breed of dog.

Meat-eaters ① ② ③

Like their wild relatives, dogs are carnivores (meat-eaters). They have strong jaws and sharp teeth for chewing. Dogs have long noses and a very good sense of smell.

Shetland sheepdog

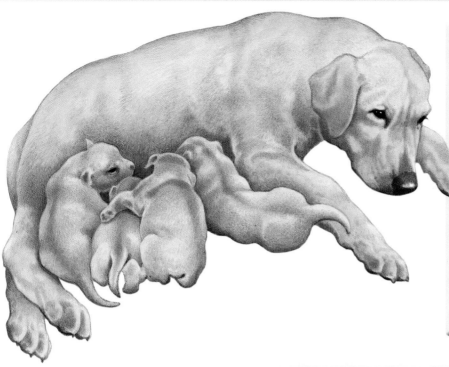

Puppies 4 5
A female dog is called a bitch. Bitches might give birth to as many as 12 puppies in a single litter. It takes two or three years for a puppy to grow to full size.

basset hound

Dalmatian

bulldog 8

fox terrier

Breeds 6 7
Dogs have lived with people for 15,000 years. Since then, people have bred them into different types, or breeds. Each breed is suited to certain jobs – border collies are good sheepdogs. A dog that is a mixture of breeds is called a mongrel.

border collie

Cats

1 Cats hunt for birds. True or false?

2 Where are a cat's claws stored?

3 How does a mother cat clean her kittens?

4 What does a happy cat do?

5 Which wild animal are pet cats closely related to?

6 Some cats are black and white. True or false?

7 What are cats with spots and blotches called?

8 Unjumble SNAPIER to spell the name of a cat breed.

Afew thousand years ago, people welcomed cats into their homes to catch mice and rats. The cats never left and they are now much-loved pets – but they still enjoy hunting!

Little hunter ① ②

Just like a lion or tiger, a pet cat is an expert hunter. It stalks birds and mice before pouncing on them. The cat has a claw on each toe. They are stored inside a sheath to keep them sharp.

Bengal

tabby

Bundles of fur ③ ④

Cats give birth to up to five babies, or kittens. After birth, the mother licks the kittens clean and then feeds them milk. Kittens like to play with balls and soft toys. These games help kittens learn how to hunt. Cats purr when they are happy.

Breeds ⑤ ⑥ ⑦

Pet cats are close relatives of African wildcats, but they look very different. Pet cats come in many types, or breeds. They have either long or short hair. Most pet cats are white, black, ginger or grey. Cats with spots and blotches are called tabbies.

longhair

⑧ Persian

LAND ANIMALS
Record breakers

1. The heaviest land animal is the African elephant. It weighs up to six tonnes.

2. The tallest animal in the world is the giraffe. Males are about 5.5 metres high.

3. Scientists think that there are 10 billion billion individual insects living at any one time.

4. The largest colony of ants is in southern Europe. It spreads into three countries and is home to seven billion ants.

5. The fastest land animal is the cheetah. It can run up to 70 kilometres per hour.

6. The smallest reptile of all is the Jaragua sphaero, a type of lizard. It is just 1.6 centimetres long.

7. The longest-living land animals are giant tortoises. They can live for 200 years.

8. The rarest mammal in the world is a ground squirrel that lives in Canada. There are only 29 left!

9. The largest hunter on land is the polar bear.

10. The smallest breed of horse is the Falabella pony. It is just 80 centimetres tall!

Chapter three
SEA CREATURES

Blue whales   60
Dolphins   62
Killer whales   64
Seals   66
Sharks   68
Wading birds   70
Penguins   72
Albatrosses   74
Record breakers
                 76

Blue whales

The blue whale is the biggest animal that has ever lived on Earth. Its eyes are the size of grapefruits, and its huge mouth could swallow a minibus!

1 Blue whales are a type of fish. True or false?

2 What is the flat part of a whale's tail called?

3 What is a blue whale as long as?

4 How much can a blue whale eat in one day?

5 What does a blue whale eat?

6 Unjumble LENABE TALSEP to name the bristles in a blue whale's mouth.

7 What is a baby whale called?

8 Find the word for a whale's nostril.

fluke

Fishy tail　1　2

Blue whales live in the sea, but they are not fish. They need to breathe air just like we do. Instead of legs, blue whales have two long flippers and a tail with two flat flukes.

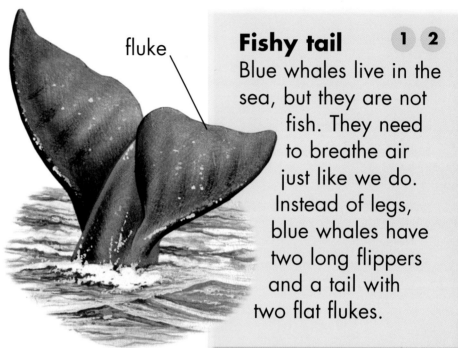

Giant of the sea　3　4

A blue whale is as long as a tennis court and weighs twice as much as a train engine. This whale can eat four tonnes of food a day.

Gulping food 5 6

Blue whales eat krill, which are like tiny shrimps. They take a gulp of water and sieve out the krill with bristles inside their mouths. The bristles are called baleen plates.

baleen plates

blowhole

Breeding 7 8

A baby whale, or calf, is born underwater. Its mother must push it to the surface so it can breathe through its huge nostrils, or blowholes.

Dolphins

There are 32 types of dolphin. Most live in groups, or pods, in warm parts of the world, far out at sea. However, a few types of dolphin live in rivers.

1 Where is a dolphin's melon?

2 The melon contains oil. True or false?

3 What does the dolphin use its melon for?

4 What is another name for a dolphin's snout?

5 What have dolphins got instead of legs?

6 Unjumble SOLRAD INF to give part of a dolphin.

7 Dolphins breathe air. True or false?

8 Dolphins never catch fish to eat. True or false?

Sound system 1 2 3

Dolphins have an oil-filled lump, known as a melon, inside their rounded heads. The melon helps them to pick up sounds underwater.

common dolphin

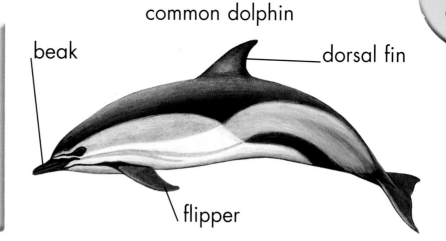

beak

dorsal fin

flipper

Body parts 4 5 6

A dolphin has a long snout, or beak, and flippers instead of legs. A fleshy dorsal fin sticks out of its back.

High jump 7 8

Dolphins often leap out of the water. They do this to breathe air and perhaps to show off. Dolphins hunt fish in groups.

Killer whales

Orcas, or killer whales, are actually a very large and powerful type of dolphin. They live in all parts of the world's oceans.

1. Do killer whales hunt for other kinds of whale?

2. What is the name of a group of killer whales?

3. Pods never contain females. True or false?

4. Which type of killer whale has a curved dorsal fin?

5. What shape is the dorsal fin of a male killer whale?

6. What happens if a fin is very tall?

7. How does a whale look around?

8. Re-arrange PSYPHPOGIN.

Hungry! ① ② ③

Killer whales hunt for seals, fish, seabirds and even other whales. Females and young whales live in groups called pods. Adult males generally live alone.

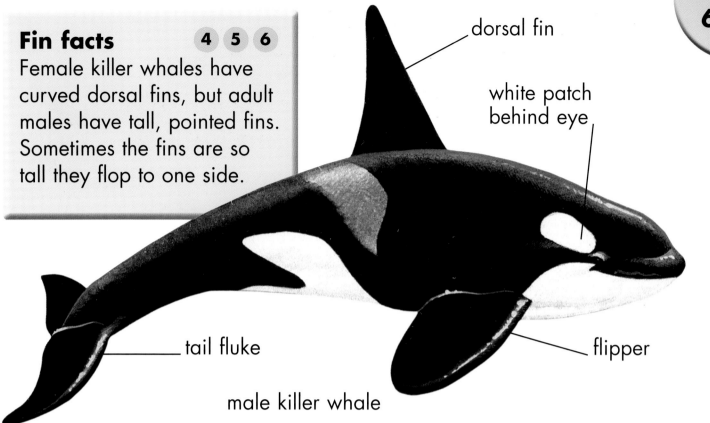

Fin facts 4 5 6
Female killer whales have curved dorsal fins, but adult males have tall, pointed fins. Sometimes the fins are so tall they flop to one side.

dorsal fin

white patch behind eye

tail fluke

flipper

male killer whale

Look out 7 8
A killer whale pokes its head out of the water so it can look around and check where it is. This is called spyhopping.

Seals

With its flippers and rounded body, a seal can only wriggle around on land. In the water, it becomes an expert swimmer.

1 Can baby seals swim?

2 Why is a baby seal's fur white?

3 Name the world's largest type of seal.

4 What is the word for a male seal?

5 Elephant seal cows are larger than the bulls. True or false?

6 Where do harp seals hunt?

7 Re-arrange LESHIFLSH to find something harp seals eat.

8 What do seals use to sense water currents made by their prey?

Hiding out
① ②
Baby seals cannot swim, and stay on land or the ice until they grow up. Their warm white fur keeps them hidden in the snow.

Sea elephants

3 4 5

The largest seal is the elephant seal. Male elephant seals, or bulls, are as big as a jeep. A bull is three times larger than a female seal, or cow.

Water hunter

6 7 8

Harp seals hunt under the ice of the Arctic Ocean. They snap up fish and shellfish. The seals' whiskers detect currents in the water made by fish.

Sharks

Sharks are the fiercest fish in the world. Many of them must swim all the time. If they stopped, they would sink to the bottom and drown.

1 What do killer sharks have in their mouths?

2 What is the largest killer shark called?

3 What does a remora use to stick itself to a shark?

4 What do pilot fish eat?

5 Can sharks detect electricity?

6 Hammerhead sharks have pointed snouts. True or false?

7 Where do blue sharks live?

8 Unjumble DQISU to spell something eaten by a shark.

Killer fish ① ②

Most sharks are hunters. They are armed with large, pointed teeth. The biggest killer of all is the great white shark. It can grow as long as a bus.

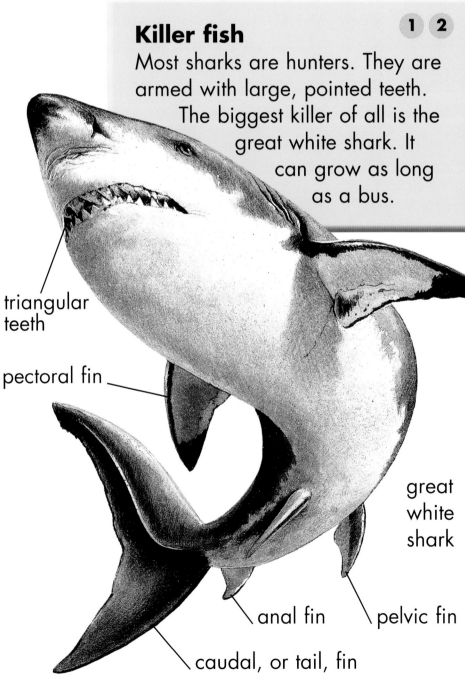

triangular teeth

pectoral fin

great white shark

anal fin

pelvic fin

caudal, or tail, fin

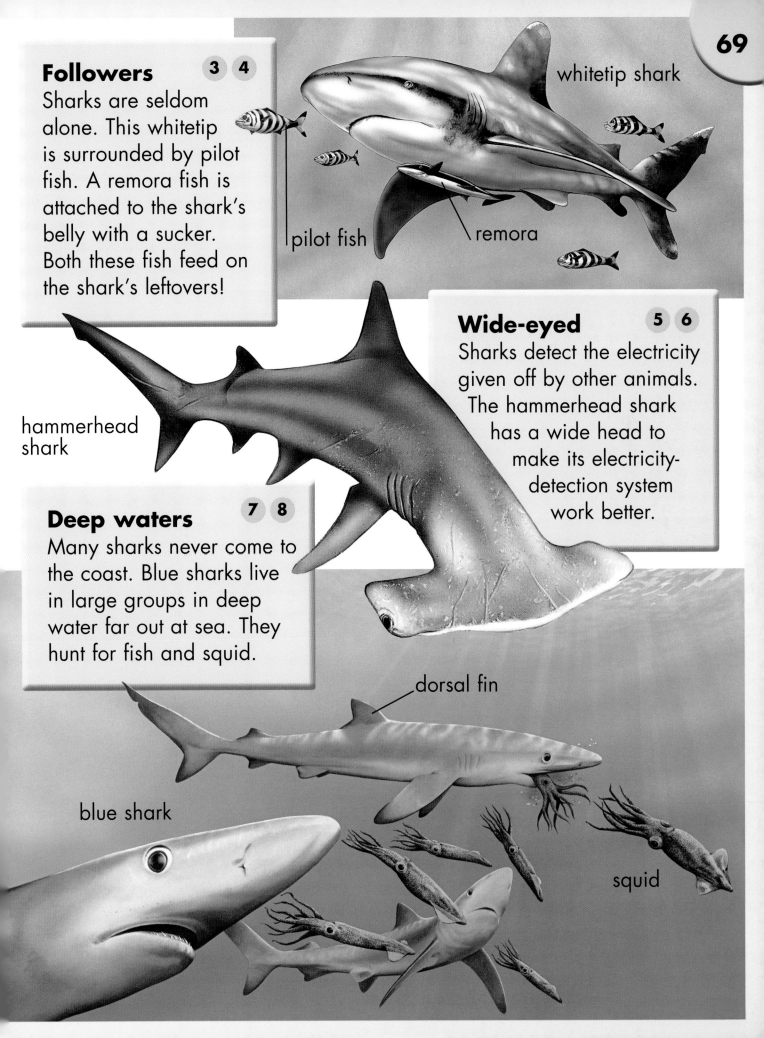

Followers ③ ④

Sharks are seldom alone. This whitetip is surrounded by pilot fish. A remora fish is attached to the shark's belly with a sucker. Both these fish feed on the shark's leftovers!

whitetip shark

pilot fish

remora

Wide-eyed ⑤ ⑥

Sharks detect the electricity given off by other animals. The hammerhead shark has a wide head to make its electricity-detection system work better.

hammerhead shark

Deep waters ⑦ ⑧

Many sharks never come to the coast. Blue sharks live in large groups in deep water far out at sea. They hunt for fish and squid.

dorsal fin

blue shark

squid

Wading birds

Shallow water is home to creatures such as worms and insects – food for wading birds! The birds catch the food with their long bills, or beaks.

1 What do spoonbills do with their beaks?

2 Where does a turnstone find food?

3 Why are a plover's eggs speckled?

4 An avocet's bill is short and flat. True or false?

5 Where does a heron stand when hunting?

6 Herons hunt for rats. True or false?

7 Unjumble ILBL to spell another word for beak.

8 A heron jumps on prey with its feet. True or false?

Waders ① ② ③ ④

A Spoonbills stir their bills in the water to attract small fish.
B Redshank
C Turnstones look for insects under pebbles.
D Plovers lay speckled eggs, which are hard to see among the pebbles.
E Black-winged stilt
F Avocets skim the surface of the water with long, curved bills.

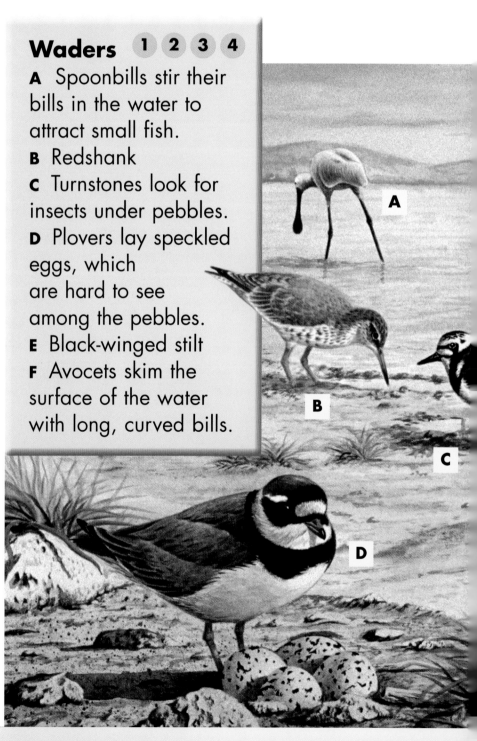

Fish hunter 5 6 7 8

A heron stands at the edge of the water and waits for a fish to swim by. With lightning speed, the heron lunges forward with its long neck and snatches the fish in its bill.

E

F

Penguins

The penguins live near Antarctica, the icy land at the South Pole. The birds cannot fly. Instead, they hunt for food underwater.

1 Unjumble RICATACNAT.

2 Where do emperor penguins keep their eggs?

3 Penguins are fast runners. True or false?

4 Do penguins ever slide over ice?

5 How do penguins swim?

6 How long can a penguin stay underwater?

7 Penguins catch fish and what other creature to eat?

8 Where do penguins find shellfish?

Hello chick! ① ②
Emperor penguins spend the winter in Antarctica as they wait for their eggs to hatch. The egg and chick are kept warm in a pouch between the legs.

Ice slide ③ ④

Penguins can only waddle on land because their legs are short. They also slide on their bellies across the ice.

Water wings ⑤ ⑥

A penguin is at home in water. The bird swims by flapping its wings as if it were flying through the water. It can dive underwater for 20 minutes.

Diving for food ⑦ ⑧

Penguins snatch fish and squid from the water and find shellfish on the sea floor.

Albatrosses

The albatross has the longest wings in the world. The distance between the wing tips is 3.5 metres – more than the height of a basketball hoop!

1 How many eggs does an albatross lay?

2 Re-arrange SAGRS to spell what nests are made from.

3 How long do the parents look after their chick?

4 Where does an albatross find food?

5 What is the bird's main food?

6 How does an albatross catch a squid?

7 Why are their wings so long?

8 How do albatrosses fly high in the sky?

Only chick ① ② ③
A female albatross lays a single egg on a nest made from a mound of grass. The mother and father raise their chick for nine months.

Scooping 4 5 6

The wandering albatross spends weeks far out at sea. It flies over the water, looking for food. Its main prey are squid, which it scoops from the surface with its strong, hooked beak.

Glider 7 8

An albatross's long wings are built for gliding. The birds ride warm winds that blow upwards. They rise as high as possible, then glide along for several days.

SEA CREATURES
Record breakers

1. The largest animal ever to live on Earth is found in the sea. The blue whale can be 30 metres long.

2. Most of the animals living in the ocean are tiny plankton. They are invisible to the naked eye.

3. The fastest animal in the ocean is the sailfish. It can swim at speeds of 110 kilometres per hour.

4. The world's largest fish is the whale shark, which grows to 14 metres long.

5. The marine iguana is the only lizard that lives in the sea.

6. The largest creature without a backbone lives in the ocean. The giant squid is 13 metres long.

7. The yellow-bellied sea snake has the most powerful venom of any snake.

8. The largest animal shell belongs to the giant clam. The shell is more than one metre tall and can weigh one quarter of a tonne.

9. The Great Barrier Reef near Australia is the only living thing that can be seen from space.

10. Seahorse fathers, not the mothers, give birth to young.

Chapter four
PEOPLE AND PLACES

Savannahs	78
Grasslands	80
Jungles	82
Mountains	84
Volcanoes	86
Earthquakes	88
Villages	90
Cities	92
On the farm	94
On the beach	96
At home	98
At school	100
Bronze Age	102
Ancient Egypt	104
Mummies	106
Buried treasure	108
Record breakers	110

Savannahs

Grassland with trees that are far apart, not close together like in a forest, is called savannah. It lies between tropical rainforests and deserts, and has rainy and sunny seasons.

1 Unjumble STEWLIEBED to spell a savannah animal.

2 Zebra stripes make them easy for lions to see. True or false?

3 Do meerkats hunt on their own?

4 Is savannah grass good for grazing?

5 Are there lots of trees on savannah?

6 What 'N' is a person who moves home regularly?

7 Is the Maasai an African tribe?

8 Do the Maasai make mud houses?

Savannah survivors ① ② ③
A Wildebeest travel long distances as part of their annual migration.
B Zebra stripes look like shadows to lions, which are colour-blind.
C Meerkats take turns to look for danger while other meerkats hunt.

Nomads ⑥ ⑦ ⑧

People who move from place to place, such as the Maasai tribe in Africa, are called nomads. They build homes from cow dung and mud.

Good grazing ④ ⑤

D Gazelles can sprint 80 kilometres per hour.

E Savannah grass is good for grazing.

F There are few trees on savannah so the grass gets lots of sun.

Grasslands

Also known as prairies, grasslands are large areas where grass and only a few trees grow. About a fifth of the Earth is covered by grassland. It feeds 800 million people.

1 Is grassland soil good for growing?

2 What is a dairy product starting with 'C'?

3 Which two crops are grown on grasslands?

4 Name the famous grassland in Argentina.

5 The Pampas are endangered. True or false?

6 Name a bird with excellent eyesight.

7 Re-arrange SINBO to name a grassland animal.

8 What does an omnivore eat?

A big farm   ① ② ③

People use the rich, fertile grassland soil for grazing cattle, sheep and goats to produce meat and dairy products, such as milk and cheese. Wheat, grain and other crops are also grown on grasslands.

Argentinian Pampas ④ ⑤

The Pampas of Argentina have a mild climate and rich soil. Horsemen called gauchos ride over the plains and tend their flocks. The Pampas are now endangered.

A

B

C

D

The grassland menu ⑥ ⑦ ⑧

A Eagles have excellent eyesight so they can spot prey while flying.
B Bison munch lots of grass.
C The coyote is an omnivore. It eats both plants and meat.
D Prairie grouse peck at seeds.

Jungles

A thick forest in a very hot, wet climate is called a jungle. About half of all the Earth's different types of plants and animals live in jungles.

1 Name an animal that works in some jungles.

2 Who cuts down the trees in the jungle?

3 Tribes live in the jungle. True or false?

4 What do some tribes make boats out of?

5 Re-arrange WOPILPEB to name a tribal weapon.

6 Jungle covers how much of our Earth?

7 Are jungles getting bigger or smaller?

8 What 'D' is the word for many trees being cut down?

Logging ① ②
Vehicles can't get through dense jungle, but elephants can. This one is pulling a tree trunk cut down by loggers, who sell them for money.

Tribes 3 4 5

Many tribes still live in jungles, although their number is falling. Some of them travel on boats made of hollowed-out trees, and hunt using a blowpipe or bows and arrows.

Shrinking jungle 6 7 8

Jungle covers about six per cent of our planet, but 50 years ago it was more than twice that. Jungles are being cut down for trees and land. This is called deforestation.

Mountains

Mountains are parts of the Earth that are much higher than the land around them. The world's highest mountain is Mount Everest, at 8,850 metres high.

1 Who climbs mountains?

2 Why do they breathe through masks?

3 What is the top of a mountain called?

4 What 'G' is a river formed out of ice?

5 Layers of rock are called what word beginning with 'S'?

6 Mountains are formed very fast. True or false?

7 Where is the forest zone?

8 Re-arrange ETRE ENLI for where the forest zone meets the cold rock.

Thin air **1** **2**
Mountaineers climb mountains for fun. The air is much thinner at high altitude, so they carry oxygen, which they breathe in through a mask.

Cool! ③ ④

The air is cool high up, so the top (or peak) of a mountain is often cold and covered in snow. Ice rivers called glaciers can form.

Crunch! ⑤ ⑥ ⑦ ⑧

Mountains are made by layers of rock (strata) moving extremely slowly over time. The lower slopes are called the forest zone. Not much grows on the cold rock above the tree line.

peak

snow line

layers of rock (strata)

⑧ tree line

forest zone

Volcanoes

here are about 1,500 active volcanoes in the world today. They look like mountains, and sometimes they erupt without any warning, blasting out dangerous gases and hot lava.

1 What 'L' gushes out of a volcano?

2 Lava is very cold. True or false?

3 Do volcanologists visit volcanoes?

4 What do volcanologists wear?

5 What forms as a cloud after an explosion?

6 Can volcanoes be the cause of earthquakes?

7 Is a tsunami an ice cream or a giant wave?

8 Unjumble GAMMA HARMBEC to find part of a volcano.

volcano

lava

Lava 1 2

When a volcano erupts, it spews out a very hot liquid called lava. Usually this lava flows slowly. Sometimes it pours out very fast, covering everything in its path.

Volcanologists 3 4

Specially trained men and women called volcanologists visit active volcanoes to study them. They take samples of lava and rock. They always wear heatproof clothing.

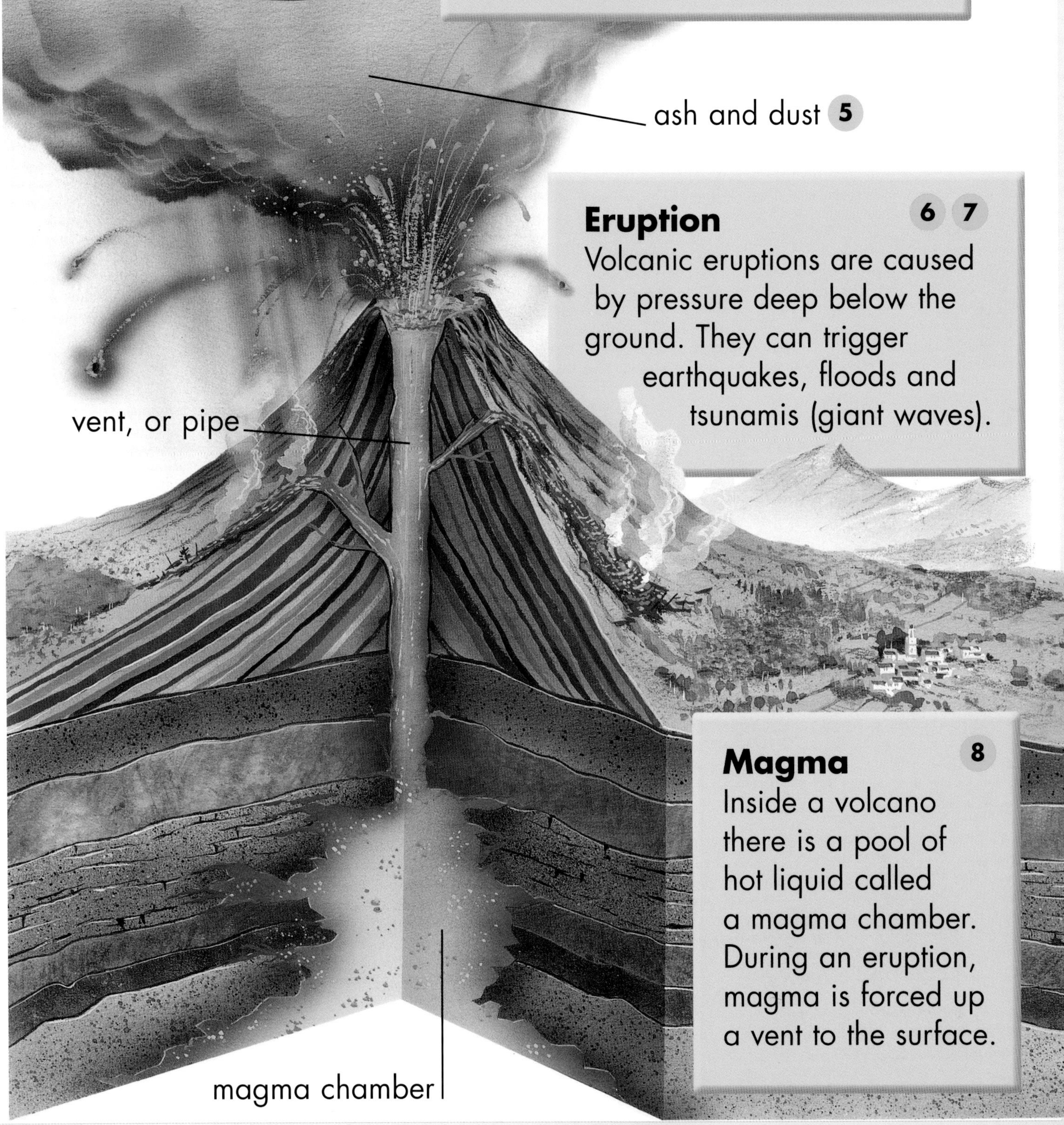

ash and dust 5

Eruption 6 7

Volcanic eruptions are caused by pressure deep below the ground. They can trigger earthquakes, floods and tsunamis (giant waves).

vent, or pipe

Magma 8

Inside a volcano there is a pool of hot liquid called a magma chamber. During an eruption, magma is forced up a vent to the surface.

magma chamber

Earthquakes

An earthquake is a sudden movement of the Earth's top layer, or crust. It makes the ground shake! Big quakes are rare, but small ones happen all the time – you can hardly feel them.

1 What 'P' are the pieces of the Earth that move very slowly over time?

2 Unjumble SERESUPR to name what builds up between the plates.

3 The Earth's crust is thick. True or false?

4 What can be cut off during a quake?

5 What might people do if their house is unsafe?

6 When did the big Tokyo quake occur?

7 What 'F' came after the Tokyo quake?

8 How many people became homeless?

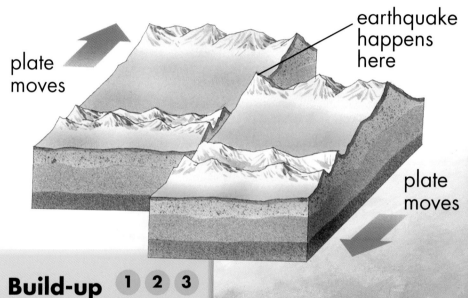

plate moves

earthquake happens here

plate moves

Build-up ① ② ③
The Earth's surface has many plates that fit together. They move very slowly over time, but if they get stuck the pressure builds up until our planet's thin crust is cracked.

Destruction 4 5

When a big earthquake occurs, buildings can be wrecked. Water and electricity supplies can also be cut off. People might move away while their houses are re-built.

Japanese disaster 6 7 8

In 1923, a huge earthquake struck near Tokyo in Japan. The quake and the fires that followed killed 142,000 people and destroyed 570,000 houses. It left 1.9 million survivors homeless.

Villages

Small settlements that are not as big as a town are called villages. Many of today's cities began as villages with houses, a place of worship and shops surrounded by farmland.

1 What are some houses built on?

2 The stilts protect them from the sun. True or false?

3 Villages are often built close to where there is what?

4 Unjumble STEMNELTET, a word for a village.

5 Where are the Atlas Mountains?

6 Name a mountain range starting with the letter 'C'.

7 Name a country beginning with 'R'.

8 Can villages be home to lots of different people?

On stilts ①②
In some villages that are near rivers, houses are built on stilts. This stops them from flooding during the rainy season.

Moroccan village (3) (4) (5)

Villages are often built where there is work. The people of this settlement in the Atlas Mountains of Morocco herd animals and grow crops.

Caucasus (6) (7) (8)

Each village dotted along the Caucasus mountain range is home to people from Russia, Armenia, Georgia and Azerbaijan. Many different languages are spoken.

Cities

1 Unjumble AGICYEMT to find the word for a very large city.

2 How many people live in a megacity?

3 Name a megacity starting with 'S'.

4 Is land in cities cheap to buy?

5 City buildings are very tall. True or false?

6 How many floors does the Sears Tower have?

7 Where were many cities first settled?

8 Why did people settle next to rivers or by the sea?

Cities are huge settlements. The biggest city by land size is New York City, USA, at 8,683 square metres. The largest by population is Tokyo, Japan, where 33 million people live.

The megacity ① ② ③

Megacities have 10 million or more inhabitants. Tokyo, below, is a megacity, and so are New York City, Mumbai, Mexico City and Shanghai.

Into the sky 4 5 6

Land is expensive in cities, so buildings are very tall to make most use of the space available. This is the view across Chicago from the Sears Tower, which has 108 floors!

Early days 7 8

Many cities were first settled next to rivers or by the sea. This was so they could receive and deliver goods by boat. Over time they expanded into cities!

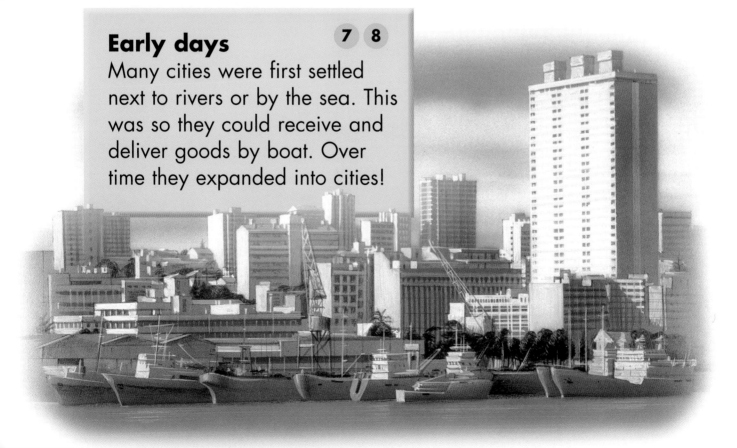

On the farm

People began farming about 10,000 years ago in the Middle East. Farms are used to breed animals, grow plants and harvest crops – we rely on them for almost all of our food.

1 Where are fruit trees planted?

2 Fruit has to be ripe before it is picked. True or false?

3 Unscramble BENMICO RETVASHER to name a farm machine.

4 When was the combine harvester invented?

5 What do combine harvesters gather?

6 Is a plough used for watering?

7 Which animal starting with 'O' pulled ploughs?

8 Which machine replaced horses?

Fruit farming   1 2
Orchards have lots of fruit trees, often planted in rows. Crops such as apples, peaches, pears and plums are picked when they are ripe.

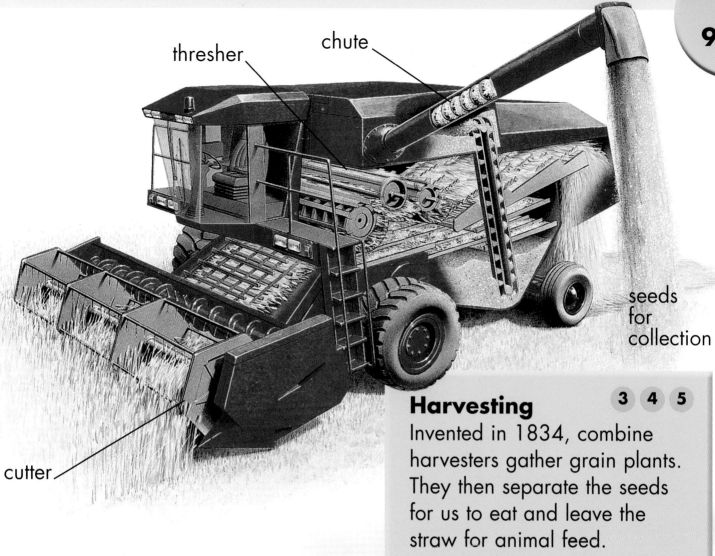

thresher

chute

seeds for collection

cutter

Harvesting 3 4 5

Invented in 1834, combine harvesters gather grain plants. They then separate the seeds for us to eat and leave the straw for animal feed.

Ploughing 6 7 8

A plough digs the soil to get it ready for planting. Since about 3500BCE, strong animals such as oxen and horses have pulled ploughs along. Now tractors do the job!

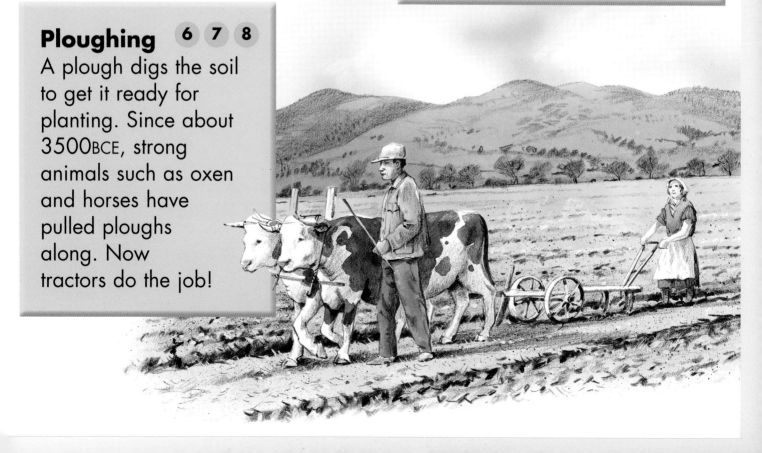

On the beach

The place where sea flows onto land is called a beach. Beaches can be made of sand, pebbles or billions of small pieces of crushed shell. There are many things to discover on a beach!

1 What happens to rockpools when the tide is out?

2 Do rockpool animals hide under umbrellas?

3 Name a bird that scavenges for food.

4 Some people eat seaweed. True or false?

5 Re-arrange LESYJIFHL to reveal a sea creature that can sting you!

6 How many legs do starfish have?

7 What can you build on the beach?

8 What should you wear at the beach?

On the rocks ① ②

A rockpool is a tiny world where plants and animals live. When the tide is out and the rockpools are no longer underwater, the animals hide under rocks and seaweed.

Beach life 3 4 5 6

A Seagulls scavenge for food.
B Seaweed is a kind of algae. Some people eat seaweed after it has been prepared.
C Jellyfish can sting you – and some kinds are poisonous!
D Starfish have five legs but hundreds of tiny tube feet.

Holidays 7 8

People go to the beach for a holiday. They can sunbathe, build sandcastles, swim and play. It is important to wear sunscreen and swim in a safe place away from strong tides.

At home

A home is a building like a house or a flat where people live, often with their family. Nearly all the 6.6 billion people in the world have a home, but some do not.

1 Name a place for children to play.

2 Do gardens need to be looked after?

3 Unscramble TARPADNRENG, a family member.

4 What 'R' is the word for people in a family?

5 What is time off from work or school called?

6 Name a home leisure activity.

7 Name something beginning with 'C' that you can do at home.

8 What can people make for a friend?

Outside the home ① ②

Houses often have gardens at the front and back. Children can play in the garden and get exercise. There are also jobs to be done, such as mowing the grass, clearing fallen leaves and looking after the plants.

Relatives 3 4

Many families are made up of different generations: children, parents, aunts, uncles and grandparents. These relatives often meet up to eat together.

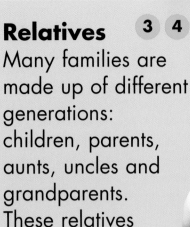

Leisure time 5 6

Time away from school or work is called leisure time. This is when people can relax and watch television, use a computer, listen to music or talk on the telephone.

Crafty time 7 8

Making art and crafts at home is a great way to spend time. People can paint, draw and cut and paste different things. They can make birthday cards for friends and photo albums of their favourite pictures.

At school

Schools are places where children learn as part of their education. They have classrooms where teachers give lessons. Schools for adults are called colleges or universities.

1. Are all schools the same?

2. What do some pupils have to help them learn?

3. Unjumble RICLUMURUC, the list of subjects taught at school.

4. Do schools teach reading and writing?

5. Maths helps you learn to use what?

6. What does science teach?

7. Why are students given tests?

8. Exam marks can be very important. True or false?

Rich and poor ① ②

There are schools all around the world, but they are not all the same. In some schools, the classes are very big and there is very little equipment for the students. In others, every pupil has their own computer.

Learning   ③ ④ ⑤ ⑥

The set of subjects taught at a school is called the curriculum. This will include reading and writing, history, sport, maths (how to use numbers) and science (how the world works).

Testing   ⑦ ⑧

Schools carry out tests, or exams, to check how much their students have learned. This is called assessment. Exam marks can be very important when children are older.

Bronze Age

This was a time when people began to use metal for tools and weapons. Its dates vary around the world, but it lasted in Europe from 2000 to 600BCE, when bronze was replaced by iron.

1 People lived in bronze houses. True or false?

2 Did their huts have a fire?

3 The hut walls were made of sticks, mud and what?

4 Unjumble RASPE to give a Bronze Age weapon.

5 Is bronze softer than gold?

6 Which two metals are mixed to make bronze?

7 What 'A' is a mix of metals?

8 What 'M' was bronze poured into while it cooled?

Smoky ① ② ③
People lived in round huts with a fire in the middle. They covered the walls with sticks, mud and dung.

axe

bracelet

sword

spear **4**

bracelet

dagger

pin

shield

axe head

brooch

Tough **5**

Bronze is much harder than gold, copper or tin. Bronze was very useful for making tools and weapons.

Hot news **6 7 8**

Bronze is made by heating tin and copper until they melt to form an 'alloy'. This liquid is poured into a mould where it cools and sets into shape.

Ancient Egypt

Ancient Egypt was a civilized kingdom for over 3,000 years, from about 3100BCE to 30BCE. It flourished on either side of the Nile river.

1 Ancient Egyptians had only one god. True or false?

2 How did priests worship the gods?

3 Most Egyptians were priests. True or false?

4 Name their important river.

5 GIRIOTRAIN is the jumbled word for managing water.

6 What 'P' was the name for an Egyptian ruler?

7 Pharaohs were thought to be half man, half what?

8 Was magic part of Egyptian life?

Many gods ① ②
Ancient Egyptians had many gods, each with different roles. Priests worshipped them by offering food and drink.

Irrigation 3 4 5

Most people were farmers who planted and harvested crops in the rich soil by the Nile river. They dug ditches to bring water to the fields — this is called irrigation.

Pharaohs 6 7 8

Rulers were called pharaohs, and they were thought to be half human, half god. Religion and magic were woven into all aspects of everyday Egyptian life.

Mummies

Ancient Egyptians believed that they would go to the afterlife after death. Their bodies would be needed there, so they were preserved, or embalmed.

1 Re-arrange LAMINBEMG, the word for preserving bodies.

2 Was embalming a fast process?

3 Was the body bandaged?

4 What happened to the brain?

5 Did everyone have many coffins?

6 How was the death mask supposed to help the spirit?

7 Coffins were left undecorated. True or false?

8 What 'S' is the name for the heavy, stone outer coffin?

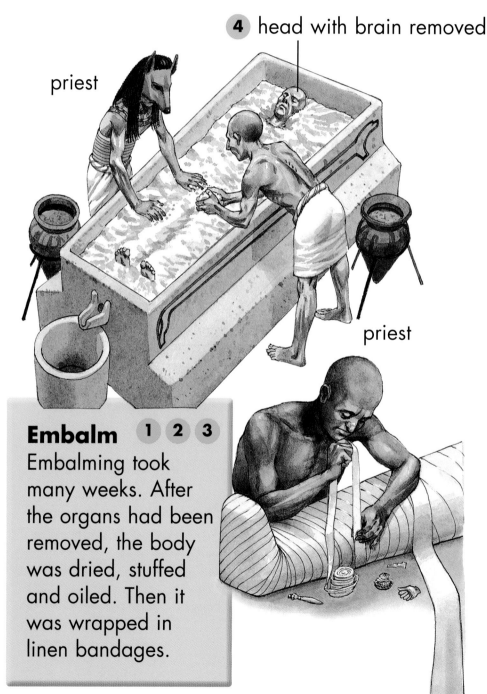

priest

4 head with brain removed

priest

Embalm 1 2 3
Embalming took many weeks. After the organs had been removed, the body was dried, stuffed and oiled. Then it was wrapped in linen bandages.

Coffins ⑤ ⑥

Only important dead people, such as pharaohs, were put inside many coffins. Some were fitted with a death mask to help the spirit recognize itself in the afterlife.

Jewels ⑦ ⑧

The internal coffins were made of wood or gold, and were painted and studded with jewels. The outer coffin was a heavy stone sarcophagus.

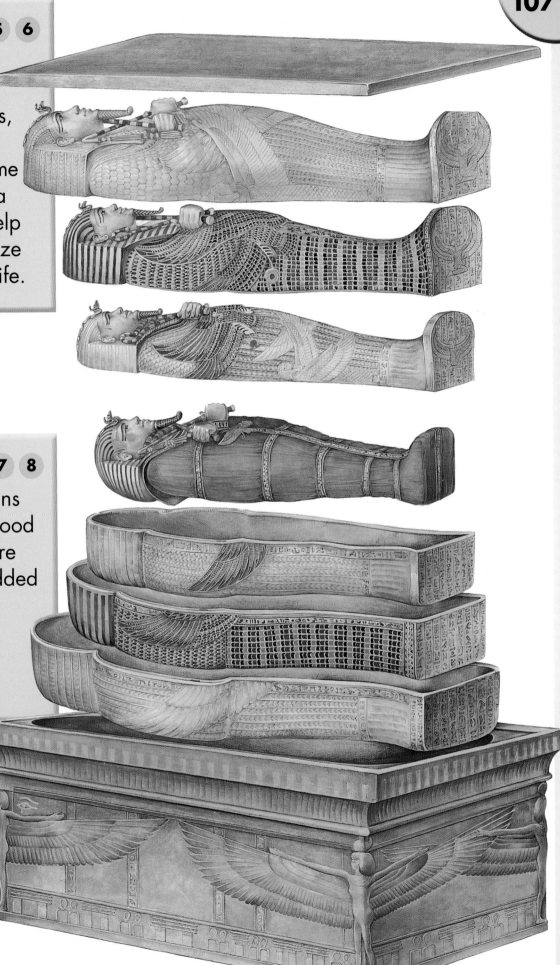

Buried treasure

Treasure is anything valuable that has been lost or hidden. In exciting movies like *Pirates of the Caribbean*, pirates look for treasure. There is lots of treasure around the world still to be found!

1 Unjumble STREEAUR PAM, which shows where treasure is buried.

2 Which letter 'marks the spot'?

3 Which famous book did R L Stevenson write?

4 Who starting with 'P' likes treasure?

5 What did pirates probably do with their treasure?

6 Which Spanish ship carried lots of precious cargo?

7 What starting with 'S' is treasure?

8 Do divers search on dry land?

Treasure maps 1 2

Treasure hunters often have a treasure map showing where the riches have been buried. The maps usually have an 'X' to mark the spot where it is hidden.

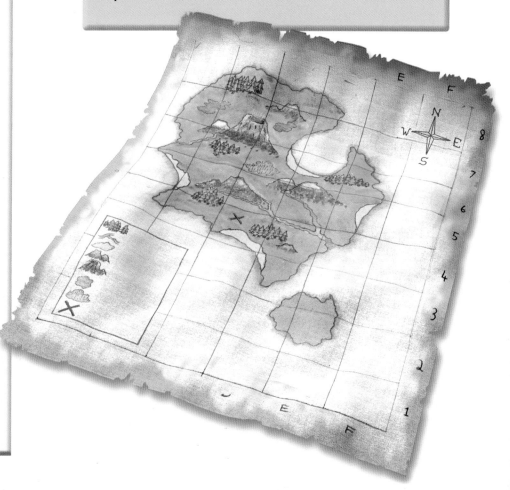

Yo ho ho! ③ ④ ⑤

Stories like Robert Louis Stevenson's *Treasure Island* suggest that pirates hid their loot in treasure chests. It is much more likely that they just spent it!

Sunken treasure ⑥ ⑦ ⑧

Over the centuries, countless ships such as Spanish galleons have sunk with their cargo of gold, silver and jewels. Divers swim down to the ocean floor hoping to find their fortune.

PEOPLE AND PLACES
Record breakers

1. The Stromboli volcano in Italy has erupted frequently for more than 2,000 years!

2. The deadliest-ever earthquake killed 830,000 people in Shaanxi, China, on 23 January 1556.

3. In 1953, Edmund Hillary and Tenzing Norgay became the first people to climb Mount Everest.

4. The Praia do Cassino in Brazil is the longest beach in the world, stretching for 254 kilometres.

5. The Maasai people value cattle as a sign of wealth rather than the amount of land owned.

6. The oldest known city is Jericho on the West Bank, where people have lived since 9000BCE.

7. The people of Africa did not have a Bronze Age – iron was the first metal to be mastered.

8. Hieroglyphic writing was developed by the ancient Egyptians in 3100BCE.

9. The ancient Egyptians were the first people to use ramps and levers – invented for pyramid building.

10. The first record of a school was in ancient Greece; it was founded in about 385BCE at Akademia.

Chapter five
TRANSPORT

Cars 112
Racing cars 114
Trucks 116
Diggers 118
Trains 120
Ships 122
Aeroplanes 124
Rockets 126
Record breakers 128

Cars

Cars are four-wheeled vehicles used for carrying people. Most run on petrol or diesel, but some run on gas, electricity or even cooking oil!

1 Has the Mini been popular for more than 40 years?

2 What is the name for a modern Mini?

3 Do Minis have four doors?

4 What does the driver use to change gear?

5 Unjumble SENDERWINC, the glass in front of the driver.

6 Do cars have only a few parts?

7 What helps control modern cars?

8 Which car was adapted from a US army vehicle?

A classic car 1 2 3
The Mini is a very famous car that has been popular for more than 40 years. Its shape has changed only a little bit and the modern Mini Cooper now has larger wheels.

1960s

MINI COOPER

2007

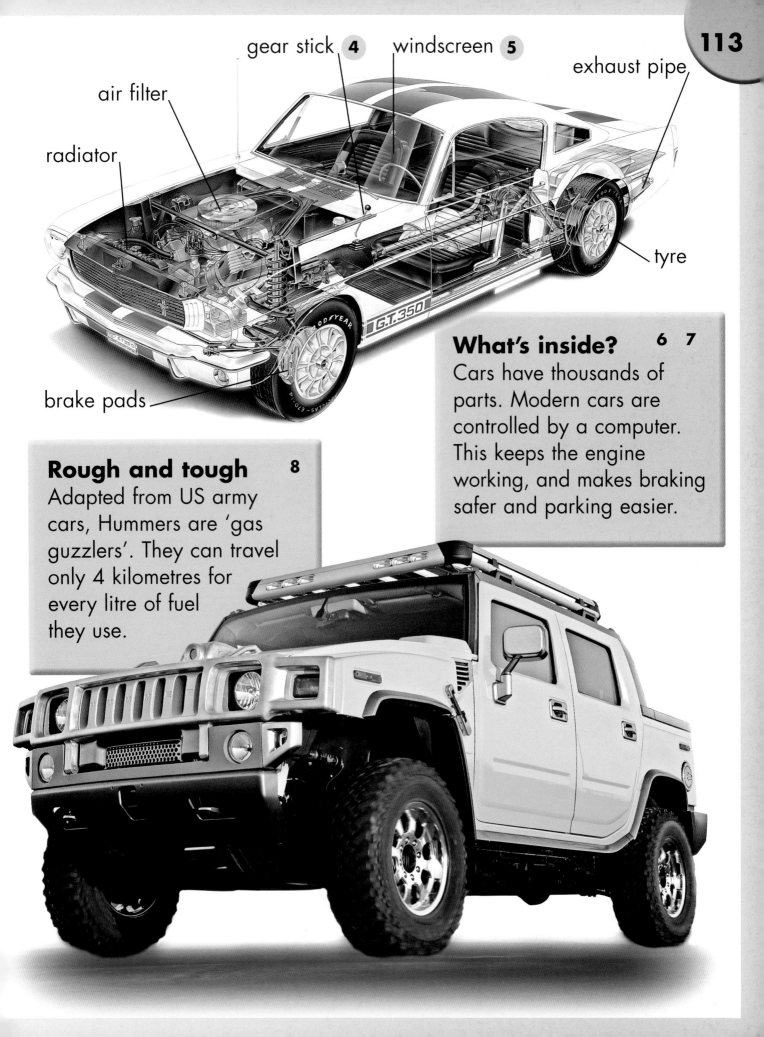

gear stick **4**   windscreen **5**

air filter

exhaust pipe

radiator

tyre

brake pads

G.T.350

What's inside?   **6**   **7**
Cars have thousands of parts. Modern cars are controlled by a computer. This keeps the engine working, and makes braking safer and parking easier.

Rough and tough   **8**
Adapted from US army cars, Hummers are 'gas guzzlers'. They can travel only 4 kilometres for every litre of fuel they use.

Racing cars

Racing cars are fast, light, single-seater cars with a powerful engine mounted behind the driver. They race at over 300 kilometres per hour.

1 Unjumble TOCCPKI.

2 How many mechanics might be in a pit crew?

3 A quick tyre change and re-fuel is known as what?

4 Is it hot in the car?

5 Drivers brake often. True or false?

6 Where are the wings on the cars?

7 What might the car do without its wings to keep it close to the road?

8 Starting with 'A', air pushing the car down is known as what?

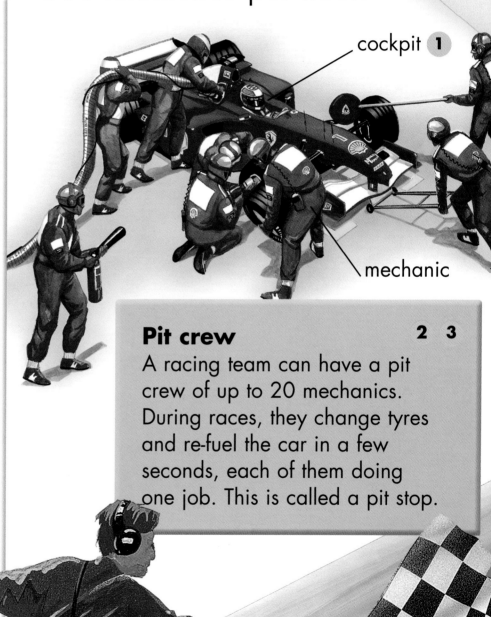

cockpit **1**

mechanic

Pit crew   **2 3**

A racing team can have a pit crew of up to 20 mechanics. During races, they change tyres and re-fuel the car in a few seconds, each of them doing one job. This is called a pit stop.

Fit and fast   4 5

Drivers have to be fit and think fast during races. They sit in a very hot cockpit and talk to their team through headphones. When they try to overtake other cars, they brake as little as possible.

Aerodynamics   6 7 8

The front and tail wings are sloped to push up air. This forces the car down, keeping it close to the road – otherwise it could crash. This is known as aerodynamics.

Trucks

Trucks deliver goods by road. Everything in your house probably came by truck. The biggest trucks can carry up to 360 tonnes!

1 Unjumble RILARET to name a part of some trucks.

2 How many parts do articulated trucks have?

3 Can articulated trucks turn easily in small spaces?

4 Do some cabs have a bed?

5 What 'C' is the rigid frame for trucks?

6 Does a lorry have a single chassis?

7 What kind of trucks carry sand?

8 Do tipper trucks have telescopic rods?

trailer **1**

trailer hitch

Two parts **2** **3** **4**
Articulated trucks have two parts – the cab and the trailer. They can turn easily in small spaces. Some have a bed for the driver to sleep in on long journeys.

van

lorry

telescopic rod

trailer

tipper truck

Rigid trucks   **5 6**

These smaller trucks have a rigid frame, called the chassis, to which the wheels and engine are attached. A lorry, unlike an articulated truck, has a single chassis. A van is like a big, boxy car.

cab

Pour me out!   **7 8**

Tipper trucks carry loose loads, such as sand or rubble. The trailer is pushed up by a telescopic rod, which is powered by oil under high pressure (this is called hydraulics). Then everything falls out, and the job is done!

Diggers

Diggers are heavy-duty vehicles. They can dig up large amounts of earth such as soil or rocks. They can move tonnes of material very quickly.

1 How do diggers scoop up earth?

2 Where does the driver sit?

3 Unjumble BAEDL to give part of a digger.

4 Are diggers used to build roads?

5 Do diggers make holes in the ground?

6 Diggers can move lots of earth. True or false?

7 Diggers are sometimes called what?

8 What helps diggers grab lots of earth at once?

crane

cables

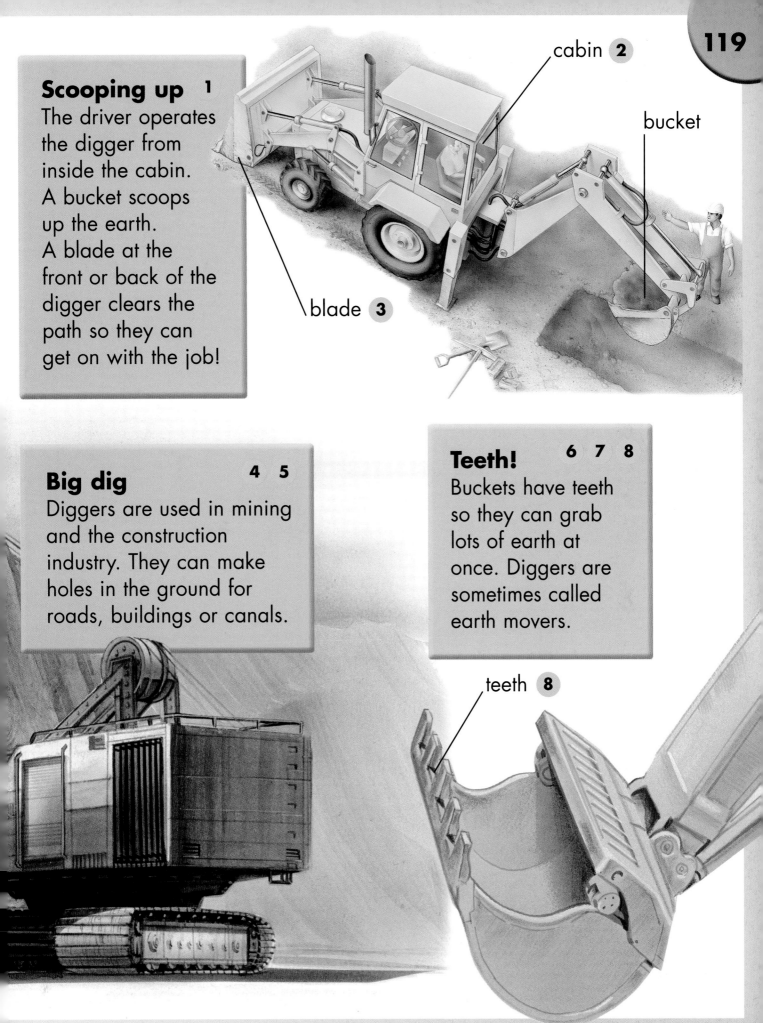

cabin **2**

bucket

Scooping up **1**

The driver operates the digger from inside the cabin. A bucket scoops up the earth. A blade at the front or back of the digger clears the path so they can get on with the job!

blade **3**

Big dig **4 5**

Diggers are used in mining and the construction industry. They can make holes in the ground for roads, buildings or canals.

Teeth! **6 7 8**

Buckets have teeth so they can grab lots of earth at once. Diggers are sometimes called earth movers.

teeth **8**

Trains

Trains have engines called locomotives that pull or push carriages along tracks made of steel rails. The first trains were invented about 200 years ago and were powered by steam.

1 How does the driver see in the dark?

2 What 'G' do freight trains carry?

3 How many wagons did the longest freight train have?

4 Do all trains have just one engine?

5 All trains are powered by diesel. True or false?

6 What comes from overhead wires?

7 Unjumble TNSOIAT to name where people get on and off.

8 How fast are the quickest trains?

driver's cab

1 headlamps

locomotive (engine)

wagon

Cargo! 2 3 4

Freight trains carry goods, not passengers. The longest-ever freight train had 660 wagons and 16 engines.

Bright spark 5 6

Many trains have diesel engines, but some are powered by electricity. They have special poles that touch overhead wires to collect the electric power.

overhead railway

People carriers 7 8

Passenger trains carry people on journeys between stations. Some have carriages where you can eat or sleep. The fastest trains, in France, can go at 574 kilometres per hour.

Ships

Ships carry passengers or goods across the seas. Once made from wood and swept along by sails, they are now built of steel and powered through the water by propellers.

1 What 'W' do warships have?

2 What are warships usually part of?

3 Which kind of ship carries goods?

4 Unjumble TONSERNAIC, which cranes lift onto the deck.

5 Some tankers carry oil. True or false?

6 Where are ships controlled from?

7 Where would you sleep on a liner?

8 How many passengers can the biggest cruise ship carry?

radar scanner

bridge

Warships 1 2
Warships are ships with weapons. They are usually part of a navy, and carry fighting equipment such as guns, cannons, torpedoes and missile launchers.

warship

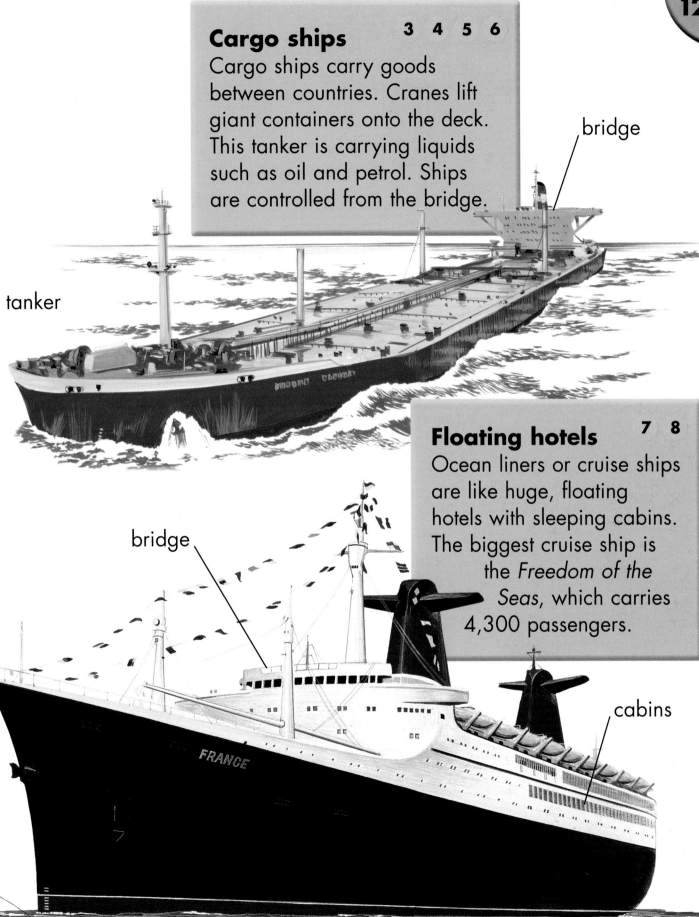

Cargo ships
3 4 5 6

Cargo ships carry goods between countries. Cranes lift giant containers onto the deck. This tanker is carrying liquids such as oil and petrol. Ships are controlled from the bridge.

bridge

tanker

Floating hotels
7 8

Ocean liners or cruise ships are like huge, floating hotels with sleeping cabins. The biggest cruise ship is the *Freedom of the Seas*, which carries 4,300 passengers.

bridge

cabins

FRANCE

ocean liner

Aeroplanes

Aeroplanes are big, heavy flying machines that carry hundreds of people and lots of cargo over long distances. Only rockets can travel faster!

1 What does a jet engine suck in at the front?

2 What helps lift the plane into the air?

3 Aeroplanes cruise at what speed?

4 Unjumble YURWAN, where planes take off.

5 Who makes sure the planes land safely?

6 Who re-fuels the planes?

7 There are different sections for people and what?

8 How many passengers can big planes carry?

Fly high   1 2 3

Jet engines suck in air at the front, and send out hot exhaust gases at the back, pushing the plane forwards. The wings have flaps that help lift the plane up into the air. Aeroplanes cruise at 700 to 900 kilometres per hour.

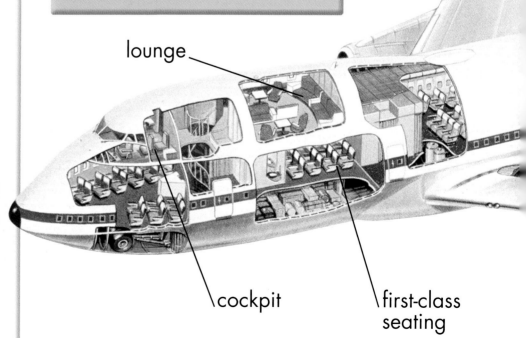

lounge

cockpit

first-class seating

Airport   4 5 6

Planes take off and land at the airport on the runway. Air-traffic controllers make sure the planes land safely. The airport ground crew do safety checks and re-fuel the planes.

economy seating

luggage

Looking inside   7 8

There are different sections inside the body of a plane for people and luggage. The largest planes can carry more than 500 passengers.

jet engine

Rockets

Rockets blast space-craft from Earth into space. They zoom into the sky at 11 kilometres per second. They are used by the military and for exploring space.

1 Are some parts meant to fall off?

2 Change LOLOPA into the craft that went to the moon.

3 Are space shuttles re-usable?

4 How many astronauts does the orbiter carry?

5 What is attached to the fuel tank for extra power?

6 Does the whole of the space shuttle go into space?

7 The fuel tank holds only 2 litres of fuel. True or false?

8 What 'P' bring the boosters back?

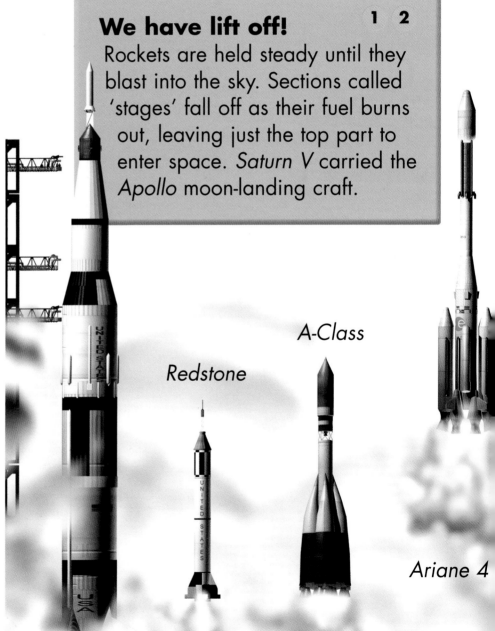

We have lift off! 1 2

Rockets are held steady until they blast into the sky. Sections called 'stages' fall off as their fuel burns out, leaving just the top part to enter space. *Saturn V* carried the *Apollo* moon-landing craft.

A-Class

Redstone

Ariane 4

Saturn V

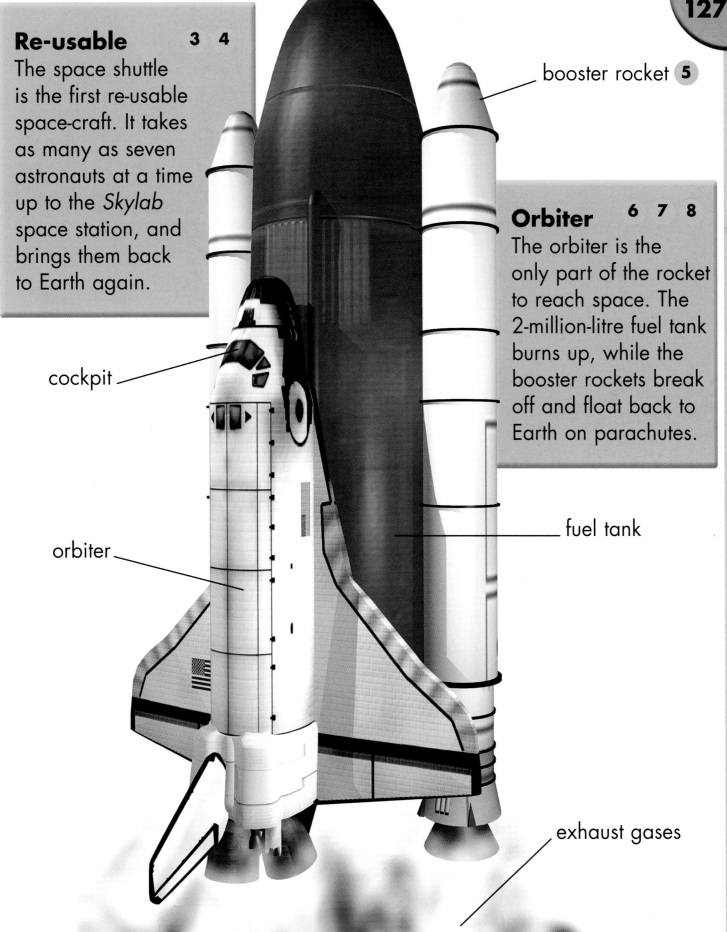

Re-usable 3 4

The space shuttle is the first re-usable space-craft. It takes as many as seven astronauts at a time up to the *Skylab* space station, and brings them back to Earth again.

booster rocket 5

Orbiter 6 7 8

The orbiter is the only part of the rocket to reach space. The 2-million-litre fuel tank burns up, while the booster rockets break off and float back to Earth on parachutes.

cockpit

orbiter

fuel tank

exhaust gases

TRANSPORT
Record breakers

1. Ferdinand Magellan led the first expedition to sail around the entire world, from 1519 to 1522.

2. The first automobile was invented by Nicolas-Joseph Cugnot in 1769.

3. The first passenger train rolled along the track on 25 March 1807 in Swansea, Wales.

4. The biggest digger is the Bagger 288, a 300-metre-long mining monster.

5. The Liebherr T282, the world's biggest truck, can carry a 360-tonne load at 64 kilometres per hour.

6. The jet-powered Thrust SSC car set a land speed record of 1,228 kilometres per hour in 1997.

7. The Lockheed SR-71A Blackbird set a record speed of 3,529 kilometres per hour for a manned plane.

8. In 1961, Yuri Gagarin became the first man to survive a trip into space and back.

9. The fastest aircraft was the pilotless Boeing X-43, which reached 12,144 kilometres per hour.

10. The longest aeroplane is the 84-metre AN-225 Mriya with wings 88 metres across and 32 wheels.

ANSWERS

Did you get it right? Now it is time to check your answers and see how well you have done! Good luck...

Dinosaurs 130

Land animals 134

Sea creatures 142

People and places 146

Transport 154

Dinosaurs

Early dinosaurs

1 What does 'dinosaur' mean?

Answer: Terrible lizard

2 All dinosaurs were small. True or false?

Answer: False. Many were large

3 How many types of dinosaur were there?

Answer: 10,000

4 Did dinosaurs lay eggs?

Answer: Yes

5 Unjumble DOOPRSAU to spell a type of dinosaur.

Answer: SAUROPOD

6 What were meat-eating dinosaurs called?

Answer: Theropods

7 Did crocodiles live at the same time as the dinosaurs?

Answer: Yes

8 How did a *Coelophysis* move?

Answer: Ran on its back legs

Meat-eaters

1 Where did the *Allosaurus* live?

Answer: North America

2 What did the *Allosaurus* use to kill prey?

Answer: Jagged teeth

3 When did the *Albertosaurus* live?

Answer: 70 million years ago

4 How did the *Albertosaurus* kill its victims?

Answer: By biting the back of the neck

5 *Deinonychus* moved slowly. True or false?

Answer: False. Deinonychus was a fast runner.

6 Did *Deinonychus* ever hunt in groups?

Answer: Yes, possibly

7 What does '*Deinonychus*' mean?

Answer: Terrible claw

8 Unjumble the word WALC.

Answer: CLAW

Tyrannosaurus rex

1 *Tyrannosaurus rex ate dead bodies. True or false?*

Answer: True

2 How did *T. rex* find dead bodies?

Answer: Sniffed them out

3 Did *T. rex* stand on four legs?

Answer: No. It stood on two legs.

4 Was *T. rex* fast?

Answer: No

5 Re-arrange GGEDAJ ETEHT to name something used by *T. rex* when hunting.

Answer: JAGGED TEETH

6 What does 'Tyrannosaurus rex' mean?

Answer: King of the tyrant lizards

7 When did *T. rex* live?

Answer: 70 million years ago

8 Where have most *T. rex* fossils been discovered?

Answer: North America

Plant-eaters

1 The *Apatosaurus* was bigger than a blue whale. True or false?

Answer: False. It was almost as large as a blue whale.

2 What is another name for the *Apatosaurus*?

Answer: Brontosaurus

3 Unjumble SUROTUESGAS.

Answer: STEGOSAURUS

4 What were the plates on a *Stegosaurus* for?

Answer: For cooling down the animal

5 What was on a *Stegosaurus*'s tail?

Answer: Spikes

6 What does 'Triceratops' mean?

Answer: Three horns

7 What are the horns of a *Triceratops* for?

Answer: To fight off predators

8 What protects a *Triceratops*'s neck?

Answer: A thick shield

Brachiosaurus

1 Unjumble ELAESV to spell food eaten by a *Brachiosaurus*.

Answer: LEAVES

2 What made their teeth blunt?

Answer: Eating leaves and branches

3 Where were its nostrils?

Answer: On top of its head

4 Nostrils may have helped their sense of smell. True or false?

Answer: True

5 What else may the nostrils have been used for?

Answer: Making loud calls

6 How heavy was a *Brachiosaurus*?

Answer: 77 tonnes

7 Which is taller, a *Brachiosaurus* or a telephone pole?

Answer: Brachiosaurus

8 How long was a *Brachiosaurus*?

Answer: 22 metres

Ancient sea reptiles

1 When did the *Archelon* live?

Answer: 220 million years ago

2 What did *Archelon* eat?

Answer: Shellfish

3 How long was an *Archelon*?

Answer: As long as a car

4 Which sea reptile looked like a dolphin?

Answer: Ichthyosaur

5 Plesiosaurs had long necks. True or false?

Answer: True

6 What did a *Placodus* eat?

Answer: Shellfish

7 What did *Globidens* crush?

Answer: Shells

8 Unjumble SAUROTHON to spell an ocean reptile with sharp teeth.

Answer: NOTHOSAUR

Flying reptiles

1 What does 'pterosaur' mean?

Answer: Winged lizard

2 Was a pterosaur's wing made of skin?

Answer: Yes

3 The wing contained a long finger. True or false?

Answer: True

4 Were pterosaurs very good at flying?

Answer: No

5 How did cliff-living pterosaurs catch their food?

Answer: By swooping over water and scooping up fish

6 Was *Dimorphodon* a fast runner?

Answer: Yes

7 Unjumble TCSNIE to spell food eaten by *Dimorphodon*.

Answer: INSECT

8 Was the largest flying animal a pterosaur?

Answer: Yes

Early mammals

1 Re-arrange SPARUMILAS.

Answer: MARSUPIALS

2 Where are marsupial babies kept after birth?

Answer: In their mother's pouch

3 Where do most marsupials live today?

Answer: Australia

4 Mammals lived at the same time as dinosaurs. True or false?

Answer: True

5 What happened when dinosaurs became extinct?

Answer: Mammals took over.

6 Did mammals eat dinosaur eggs?

Answer: Yes, possibly

7 Dinosaurs had hair. True or false?

Answer: False. Mammals have hair.

8 Does a mammal's hair keep it warm?

Answer: Yes

Land animals

Elephants

1 What is a group of elephants called?

Answer: A herd

2 Are male elephants in charge of the herd?

Answer: No. The females are in charge.

3 What is an elephant's tusk made of?

Answer: Ivory

4 Can you train an elephant to work?

Answer: Yes

5 Unjumble NALABINH to spell a famous general's name.

Answer: HANNIBAL

6 Do elephants eat leaves and grass?

Answer: Yes

7 Elephants eat for 16 hours a day. True or false?

Answer: True

8 Are plants a high-energy food?

Answer: No

Lions

1 What is the thick hair on a lion's neck called?

Answer: A mane

2 Male and female lions are the same size. True or false?

Answer: False. The male is larger.

3 What is a group of lions called?

Answer: A pride

4 Who rules a group of lions?

Answer: A male lion

5 What are baby lions called?

Answer: Cubs

6 Which member of the pride always eats first?

Answer: The male leader

7 Unjumble SENOSIL to work out who raises a baby lion.

Answer: LIONESS

8 What does a male lion do if he meets another male?

Answer: Fight

Tigers

1 Why do tigers have stripes?

Answer: Helps them stay hidden

2 Do tigers make much noise when they walk?

Answer: No

3 Unjumble RIGESTS to give the word for a female tiger.

Answer: TIGRESS

4 How long does a tiger cub stay with its mother?

Answer: Two years

5 Tigers live in large groups. True or false?

Answer: False. Tigers live alone.

6 How do tigers keep their claws sharp?

A: By scratching tree trunks

7 How does a tiger get close to prey?

Answer: Hides in the undergrowth and creeps up

8 How do tigers kill their prey?

Answer: Break their neck

Wolves

1 Which small animal might a wolf catch?

Answer: A hare

2 When do wolves hunt as a team?

Answer: Winter

3 Unjumble NURNGIN to give something wolves are very good at.

Answer: RUNNING

4 How far can a wolf run in a day?

Answer: 200 kilometres

5 A group of wolves is called a flock. True or false?

Answer: False. It is called a pack.

6 How many pack members have cubs each year?

Answer: Two

7 Why do wolves howl?

Answer: To warn other wolves to stay away.

8 How far away can you hear a wolf howling?

Answer: 16 kilometres

Flightless birds

1 Cassowaries live in the desert. True or false?

Answer: False. They live in forests.

2 Unjumble SQAECU to name the bone on a cassowary's head.

Answer: CASQUE

3 What is the cassowary's casque used for?

Answer: To push branches out of the way.

4 What is the largest bird in the world?

Answer: The ostrich

5 Where do ostriches live?

Answer: Africa

6 How does an ostrich escape from danger?

Answer: By running away

7 How did the emu get its name?

Answer: From the call it makes

8 How does an emu find fresh food?

Answer: Follows the rain clouds

Bears

1 How do bears climb trees?

Answer: By gripping with their claws

2 How long are the claws of a brown bear?

Answer: 10 centimetres long

3 Unjumble EVEEBIH for the place where bears find honey.

Answer: BEEHIVE

4 Bears never eat fish. True or false?

Answer: False. They eat salmon and trout.

5 Where do bears often gather to catch fish?

Answer: Waterfalls

6 Bears can catch fish with their teeth. True or false?

Answer: True

7 Do bears like to eat nuts and berries?

Answer: Yes

8 How do bears eat honey?

Answer: Lick it out with their tongues

Pandas

1 Why do pandas have white faces with black eyes and ears?

Answer: To make it easier to see each other in the forest.

2 Re-arrange OBAMOB for the plant pandas eat.

Answer: BAMBOO

3 Where do pandas sleep?

Answer: In the open

4 What sticks out of a panda's wrist?

Answer: A sixth 'finger'

5 How long does it take for a panda cub to grow up?

Answer: Four years

6 Which country do pandas live in?

Answer: China

7 How many pandas live in the wild?

Answer: 1,000

8 Do pandas live on mountains?

Answer: Yes

Polar bears

1 Is a polar bear's hair white?

Answer: No. It is see-through.

2 Why do bears store a layer of fat under the skin?

Answer: So they can survive if they cannot find food

3 Unjumble END to name the place cubs are born.

Answer: DEN

4 How long do cubs stay in the den?

Answer: Three months

5 What does a polar bear mother eat when she is in the den with her cubs?

Answer: Nothing

6 What do polar bears hunt?

Answer: Seals

7 Where do they wait for prey?

Answer: Next to holes in the ice

8 Polar bears catch seals with fishing rods. True or false?

Answer: False. They use their paws.

Jungle animals

1 Why are jungles being cut down?

Answer: *To make room for farms.*

2 Why are some jungle animals rare?

Answer: *They have few places left to live.*

3 Unjumble VAJNA to spell the name of a rare rhino.

Answer: *JAVAN*

4 How many horns does a Javan rhino have?

Answer: *One*

5 How do toucans crack nuts?

Answer: With their big beaks.

6 How long is a quetzal's tail?

Answer: *Four times longer than the rest of its body.*

7 What would happen if someone touched the red frog?

Answer: *They might die.*

8 Where does the ocelot hunt?

Answer: *In the undergrowth*

Apes and monkeys

1 Where could you find a wild gorilla?

Answer: *Africa*

2 Which ape lives in southeast Asia?

Answer: *The orang-utan*

3 What is the most common type of ape in the world?

Answer: *The human*

4 When do howler monkeys call?

Answer: *In the morning*

5 How far away can a howler monkey's call be heard?

Answer: *Three kilometres*

6 Where is the howler monkey's voicebox?

Answer: *In its throat*

7 Unjumble DRIMLALN to spell the name of the largest monkey.

Answer: *MANDRILL*

8 Where do mandrills live?

Answer: *The jungles of Africa*

Bugs and beetles

1 What do bugs have instead of bones?

Answer: Hard skin

2 How do bugs breathe?

Answer: Through holes in their skin

3 A water bug has hairy legs to keep warm. True or false?

Answer: False. Its hairy legs help it swim.

4 How do water bugs catch fish?

Answer: With their long claws

5 What do stag beetles use their pincers for?

Answer: Fighting

6 Unjumble NATENANE for insect feelers.

Answer: ANTENNAE

7 How many legs does a bug have?

Answer: Six

8 Where do beetles keep their wings?

Answer: Underneath a hard wing case

Ants

1 Where do weaver ants live?

Answer: In a nest of leaves

2 Baby ants are called larvae. True or false?

Answer: True

3 What do larvae make to glue leaves together?

Answer: Sticky silk

4 Which ants defend the nest?

Answer: Soldier ants

5 Soldier ants are armed with sharp jaws, and what other weapon?

Answer: Stingers in their tails

6 Where might you find an ant nest?

Answer: Underground

7 Which type of ant gathers food?

A: Worker ants

8 Unjumble UPAPE to find the name for ant cocoons.

Answer: PUPAE

Butterflies and moths

1 What hatches from a butterfly egg?

Answer: A caterpillar

2 What do caterpillars eat?

Answer: Leaves and fruit

3 What is the name of the silk bag that a caterpillar spins?

Answer: A cocoon

4 Unjumble CRAMNOH to spell the name of a common butterfly.

Answer: MONARCH

5 Moths fly at night. True or false?

Answer: True

6 Which are more colourful, moths or butterflies?

Answer: Butterflies

7 How many wings do butterflies have?

Answer: Four (two pairs)

8 What is the mouthpart of a butterfly called?

Answer: A proboscis

Farm animals

1 Cockerels lay eggs. True or false?

Answer: False. Hens lay eggs.

2 What is a female chicken called?

Answer: A hen

3 Where does wool come from?

Answer: Sheep

4 Which breed of cattle is best for producing milk?

Answer: Jersey

5 Unjumble FROHEERD to spell the name of a cattle breed.

Answer: HEREFORD

6 What is special about Highland cattle?

Answer: Their thick hair

7 Ham, pork and what other meat comes from a pig?

Answer: Bacon

8 What is a female pig called?

Answer: A sow

Dogs

1 What does 'carnivore' mean?

Answer: Meat-eater

2 What does a dog use its teeth for?

Answer: Chewing

3 Dogs have no sense of smell. True or false?

Answer: False. Dogs have a good sense of smell.

4 How many puppies can a bitch produce?

Answer: Up to 12

5 How long do puppies take to become adults?

Answer: Two or three years

6 When did dogs start to live with people?

Answer: 15,000 years ago

7 What is a mongrel?

Answer: A mixed-breed dog

8 Unjumble GOBDULL to spell a breed of dog.

Answer: BULLDOG

Cats

1 Cats hunt for birds. True or false?

Answer: True

2 Where are a cat's claws stored?

Answer: Inside a sheath on its toe

3 How does a mother cat clean her kittens?

Answer: By licking them

4 What does a happy cat do?

Answer: It purrs

5 Which wild animal are pet cats closely related to?

Answer: African wildcat

6 Some cats are black and white. True or false?

Answer: True

7 What are cats with spots and blotches called?

Answer: Tabbies

8 Unjumble SNAPIER to spell the name of a cat breed.

Answer: PERSIAN

Sea creatures

Blue whales

1 Blue whales are a type of fish. True or false?

Answer: False. They live in the sea, but they are not a type of fish.

2 What is the flat part of a whale's tail called?

Answer: Fluke

3 What is a blue whale as long as?

Answer: A tennis court

4 How much can a blue whale eat in one day?

Answer: Four tonnes of food

5 What does a blue whale eat?

Answer: Krill

6 Unjumble LENABE TALSEP to name the bristles in a blue whale's mouth.

Answer: BALEEN PLATES

7 What is a baby whale called?

Answer: A calf

8 Find the word for a whale's nostril.

Answer: Blowhole

Dolphins

1 Where is a dolphin's melon?

Answer: Inside its head

2 The melon contains oil. True or false?

Answer: True

3 What does the dolphin use its melon for?

Answer: To pick up sounds underwater

4 What is another name for a dolphin's snout?

Answer: Beak

5 What have dolphins got instead of legs?

Answer: Flippers

6 Unjumble SOLRAD INF to give part of a dolphin.

Answer: DORSAL FIN

7 Dolphins breathe air. True or false?

A: True

8 Dolphins never catch fish to eat. True or false?

Answer: False. They do catch fish to eat.

Killer whales

1 Do killer whales hunt for other kinds of whale?

Answer: Yes

2 What is the name of a group of killer whales?

Answer: A pod

3 Pods never contain females. True or false?

Answer: False. Females do live in pods.

4 Which type of killer whale has a curved dorsal fin?

Answer: Female killer whales

5 What shape is the dorsal fin of a male killer whale?

Answer: Tall and pointed

6 What happens if a fin is very tall?

Answer: It can flop to one side.

7 How does a whale look around?

Answer: By poking its head out of the water

8 Re-arrange PSYPHPOGIN.

Answer: SPYHOPPING

Seals

1 Can baby seals swim?

Answer: No

2 Why is a baby seal's fur white?

Answer: So it can hide in the snow

3 Name the world's largest type of seal.

Answer: Elephant seal

4 What is the word for a male seal?

Answer: Bull

5 Elephant seal cows are larger than the bulls. True or false?

Answer: False. Elephant seal bulls are larger than the cows.

6 Where do harp seals hunt?

Answer: Under the ice in the Arctic Ocean

7 Re-arrange LESHIFLSH to find something harp seals eat.

Answer: SHELLFISH

8 What do seals use to sense water currents made by their prey?

Answer: Their whiskers

Sharks

1 What do killer sharks have in their mouths?

Answer: Large, pointed teeth

2 What is the largest killer shark called?

Answer: The great white shark

3 What does a remora use to stick itself to a shark?

Answer: A sucker

4 What do pilot fish eat?

Answer: The shark's leftovers

5 Can sharks detect electricity?

Answer: Yes

6 Hammerhead sharks have pointed snouts. True or false?

Answer: False. They have wide heads.

7 Where do blue sharks live?

Answer: Far out at sea

8 Unjumble DQISU to spell something eaten by a shark.

Answer: SQUID

Wading birds

1 What do spoonbills do with their beaks?

Answer: Stir the water to attract fish

2 Where does a turnstone find food?

Answer: Under pebbles

3 Why are a plover's eggs speckled?

Answer: So that the eggs are hard to see among the pebbles.

4 An avocet's bill is short and flat. True or false?

Answer: False. Its bill is long and curved.

5 Where does a heron stand when hunting?

Answer: At the edge of the water

6 Herons hunt for rats. True or false?

Answer: False. Herons hunt for fish.

7 Unjumble ILBL to spell another word for beak.

Answer: BILL.

8 A heron jumps on prey with its feet. True or false?

Answer: False. It catches fish in its bill.

Penguins

1 Unjumble RICATACNAT.

Answer: ANTARCTICA

2 Where do emperor penguins keep their eggs?

Answer: In a pouch between their legs

3 Penguins are fast runners. True or false?

Answer: False. They can only waddle because their legs are short.

4 Do penguins ever slide over ice?

Answer: Yes

5 How do penguins swim?

Answer: By flapping their wings as if they were flying

6 How long can a penguin stay underwater?

Answer: 20 minutes

7 Penguins catch fish and what other creature to eat?

Answer: Squid

8 Where do penguins find shellfish?

Answer: On the sea floor

Albatrosses

1 How many eggs does an albatross lay?

Answer: One

2 Re-arrange SAGRS to spell what nests are made from.

Answer: GRASS

3 How long do the parents look after their chick?

Answer: Nine months

4 Where does an albatross find food?

Answer: Far out at sea

5 What is the bird's main food?

Answer: Squid

6 How does an albatross catch a squid?

Answer: It scoops it from the surface of the water with its beak.

7 Why are their wings so long?

Answer: So they can glide

8 How do albatrosses fly high in the sky?

Answer: By riding warm winds that blow upwards

People and places

Savannahs

1 Unjumble STEWLIEBED to spell a savannah animal.

Answer: WILDEBEEST

2 Zebra stripes make them easy for lions to see. True or false?

Answer: False. It makes them look like shadows to the colour-blind lions.

3 Do meerkats hunt on their own?

Answer: No

4 Is savannah grass good for grazing?

Answer: Yes

5 Are there lots of trees on savannah?

Answer: No

6 What 'N' is a person who moves home regularly?

Answer: Nomad

7 Is the Maasai an African tribe?

Answer: Yes

8 Do the Maasai make mud houses?

Answer: Yes

Grasslands

1 Is grassland soil good for growing?

Answer: Yes

2 What is a dairy product starting with 'C'?

Answer: Cheese

3 Which two crops are grown on grasslands?

Answer: Wheat and grain

4 Name the famous grassland in Argentina.

Answer: The Pampas

5 The Pampas are endangered. True or false?

Answer: True

6 Name a bird with excellent eyesight.

Answer: Eagle

7 Re-arrange SINBO to name a grassland animal.

Answer: BISON

8 What does an omnivore eat?

Answer: Both plants and meat

Jungles

1 Name an animal that works in some jungles.

Answer: Elephant

2 Who cuts down the trees in the jungle?

Answer: Loggers

3 Tribes live in the jungle. True or false?

Answer: True

4 What do some tribes make boats out of?

Answer: Hollowed-out trees

5 Re-arrange WOPILPEB to name a tribal weapon.

Answer: BLOWPIPE

6 Jungle covers how much of our Earth?

Answer: Six per cent

7 Are jungles getting bigger or smaller?

Answer: Smaller

8 What 'D' is the word for many trees being cut down?

Answer: Deforestation

Mountains

1 Who climbs mountains?

Answer: Mountaineers

2 Why do they breathe through masks?

Answer: They need oxygen because the air is thinner at high altitude.

3 What is the top of a mountain called?

Answer: Peak

4 What 'G' is a river formed out of ice?

Answer: Glacier

5 Layers of rock are called what word beginning with 'S'?

Answer: Strata

6 Mountains are formed very fast. True or false?

Answer: False. They are made by layers of rock moving slowly over time.

7 Where is the forest zone?

Answer: On the lower slopes

8 Re-arrange ETRE ENLI for where the forest zone meets the cold rock.

Answer: TREE LINE

Volcanoes

1 What 'L' gushes out of a volcano?

Answer: Lava

2 Lava is very cold. True or false?

Answer: False. It is a very hot liquid.

3 Do volcanologists visit volcanoes?

Answer: Yes

4 What do volcanologists wear?

Answer: Heatproof clothing

5 What forms as a cloud after an explosion?

Answer: Ash and dust

6 Can volcanoes be the cause of earthquakes?

Answer: Yes

7 Is a tsunami an ice cream or a giant wave?

Answer: A giant wave

8 Unjumble GAMMA HARMBEC to find part of a volcano.

Answer: MAGMA CHAMBER

Earthquakes

1 What 'P' are the pieces of the Earth that move very slowly over time?

Answer: Plates

2 Unjumble SERESUPR to name what builds up between the plates.

Answer: PRESSURE

3 The Earth's crust is thick. True or false?

Answer: False. It is thin.

4 What can be cut off during a quake?

Answer: Water and electricity

5 What might people do if their house is unsafe?

Answer: Move away while their house is rebuilt

6 When did the big Tokyo quake occur?

Answer: 1923

7 What 'F' came after the Tokyo quake?

Answer: Fires

8 How many people became homeless?

Answer: 1.9 million

Villages

1 What are some houses built on?

Answer: Stilts

2 The stilts protect them from the sun. True or false?

Answer: False. Stilts protect them when rivers flood.

3 Villages are often built close to where there is what?

Answer: Work

4 Unjumble STEMNELTET, a word for a village.

Answer: SETTLEMENT

5 Where are the Atlas Mountains?

Answer: Morocco

6 Name a mountain range starting with the letter 'C'.

Answer: Caucasus

7 Name a country beginning with 'R'.

Answer: Russia

8 Can villages be home to lots of different people?

Answer: Yes

Cities

1 Unjumble AGICYEMT to find the word for a very large kind of city.

Answer: MEGACITY

2 How many people live in a megacity?

Answer: 10 million or more

3 Name a megacity starting with 'S'.

Answer: Shanghai

4 Is land in cities cheap to buy?

Answer: No

5 City buildings are very tall. True or false?

Answer: True

6 How many floors does the Sears Tower have?

Answer: 108

7 Where were many cities first settled?

Answer: Next to rivers or by the sea.

8 Why did people settle next to rivers or by the sea?

Answer: So they could receive and deliver goods by boat

On the farm

1 Where are fruit trees planted?

Answer: Orchards

2 Fruit has to be ripe before it is picked. True or false?

Answer: True

3 Unscramble BENMICO RETVASHER to name a farm machine.

Answer: COMBINE HARVESTER

4 When was the combine harvester invented?

Answer: 1834

5 What do combine harvesters gather?

Answer: Grain plants

6 Is a plough used for watering?

Answer: No. It digs the soil.

7 Which animal starting with 'O' pulled ploughs?

Answer: Oxen

8 Which machine replaced horses?

Answer: Tractor

On the beach

1 What happens to rockpools when the tide is out?

Answer: They are no longer underwater.

2 Do rockpool animals hide under umbrellas?

Answer: No

3 Name a bird that scavenges for food.

Answer: Seagull

4 Some people eat seaweed. True or false?

A: True

5 Re-arrange LESYJIFHL to reveal a sea creature that can sting you!

Answer: JELLYFISH

6 How many legs do starfish have?

Answer: Five

7 What can you build on the beach?

Answer: Sandcastles

8 What should you wear at the beach?

Answer: Sunscreen

At home

1 Name a place for children to play.

Answer: Garden

2 Do gardens need to be looked after?

Answer: Yes

3 Unscramble TARPADNRENG, a family member.

Answer: GRANDPARENT

4 What 'R' is the word for people in a family?

Answer: Relatives

5 What is time away from work or school called?

Answer: Leisure time

6 Name a home leisure activity.

Answer: Watching television, listening to music or talking on the telephone

7 Name something beginning with 'C' that you can do at home.

Answer: Crafts

8 What can people make for a friend?

Answer: Birthday cards and photo albums.

At school

1 Are all schools the same?

Answer: No

2 What do some pupils have to help them learn?

Answer: Computers

3 Unjumble RICLUMURUC, the list of subjects taught at school.

Answer: CURRICULUM

4 Do schools teach reading and writing?

Answer: Yes

5 Maths helps you learn to use what?

Answer: Numbers

6 What does science teach?

Answer: How the world works

7 Why are students given tests?

Answer: To find out how much they have learned.

8 Exam marks can be very important. True or false?

Answer: True

Bronze Age

1 People lived in bronze houses. True or false?

Answer: False. They lived in huts.

2 Did their huts have a fire?

Answer: Yes

3 The hut walls were made of sticks, mud and what?

Answer: Dung

4 Unjumble RASPE to give a Bronze Age weapon.

Answer: SPEAR

5 Is bronze softer than gold?

Answer: No

6 Which two metals are mixed to make bronze?

Answer: Copper and tin

7 What 'A' is a mix of metals?

Answer: Alloy

8 What 'M' was bronze poured into while it cooled?

Answer: Mould

Ancient Egypt

1 Ancient Egyptians had only one god. True or false?

Answer: False. They had many gods.

2 How did priests worship the gods?

Answer: By offering them food and drink

3 Most Egyptians were priests. True or false?

Answer: False. Most were farmers

4 Name their important river.

Answer: Nile

5 GIRIOTRAIN is the jumbled word for managing water.

Answer: IRRIGATION

6 What 'P' was the name for an Egyptian ruler?

Answer: Pharaoh

7 Pharaohs were thought to be half man, half what?

Answer: God

8 Was magic part of Egyptian life?

Answer: Yes

Mummies

1 Re-arrange LAMINBEMG, the word for preserving bodies.

Answer: EMBALMING

2 Was embalming a fast process?

Answer: No

3 Was the body bandaged?

Answer: Yes

4 What happened to the brain?

Answer: It was removed.

5 Did everyone have many coffins?

Answer: No

6 How was the death mask supposed to help the spirit?

Answer: So the spirit could recognize the body in the afterlife

7 Coffins were left undecorated. True or false?

Answer: False. They were painted and decorated with jewels.

8 What 'S' is the name for the heavy, stone outer coffin?

Answer: Sarcophagus

Buried treasure

1 Unjumble STREEAUR PAM, which shows where treasure is buried.

Answer: TREASURE MAP

2 Which letter 'marks the spot'?

Answer: X

3 Which famous book did R L Stevenson write?

Answer: Treasure Island

4 Who starting with 'P' likes treasure?

Answer: Pirates

5 What did pirates probably do with their treasure?

Answer: Spend it

6 Which Spanish ship carried lots of precious cargo?

Answer: Spanish galleon

7 What starting with 'S' is treasure?

Answer: Silver

8 Do divers search on dry land?

Answer: No

Transport

Cars

1 Has the Mini been popular for more than 40 years?

Answer: Yes

2 What is the name for a modern Mini?

Answer: Mini Cooper

3 Do Minis have four doors?

Answer: No. They have only two.

4 What does the driver use to change gear?

Answer: Gear stick

5 Unjumble SENDERWINC, the glass in front of the driver.

Answer: WINDSCREEN

6 Do cars have only a few parts?

Answer: No

7 What helps control modern cars?

Answer: A computer

8 Which car was adapted from a US army vehicle?

Answer: The Hummer

Racing cars

1 Unjumble TOCCPKI.

Answer: COCKPIT

2 How many mechanics might be in a pit crew?

Answer: Up to 20

3 A quick tyre change and re-fuel is known as what?

Answer: A pit stop

4 Is it hot in the car?

Answer: Yes

5 Drivers brake often. True or false?

Answer: False. They brake as little as possible.

6 Where are the wings on the cars?

Answer: On the front and tail of the car

7 What might the car do without its wings to keep it close to the road?

Answer: Crash

8 Starting with 'A', air pushing the car down is known as what?

Answer: Aerodynamics

Trucks

1 Unjumble RILARET to name a part of some trucks.

Answer: TRAILER

2 How many parts do articulated trucks have?

Answer: Two

3 Can articulated trucks turn easily in small spaces?

Answer: Yes

4 Do some cabs have a bed?

Answer: Yes

5 What 'C' is the rigid frame for trucks?

Answer: Chassis

6 Does a lorry have a single chassis?

Answer: Yes

7 What kind of trucks carry sand?

Answer: Tipper trucks

8 Do tipper trucks have telescopic rods?

Answer: Yes

Diggers

1 How do diggers scoop up earth?

Answer: With a bucket

2 Where does the driver sit?

Answer: In the cabin

3 Unjumble BAEDL to give part of a digger.

Answer: BLADE

4 Are diggers used to build roads?

Answer: Yes

5 Do diggers make holes in the ground?

Answer: Yes

6 Diggers can move lots of earth. True or false?

Answer: True

7 Diggers are sometimes called what?

Answer: Earth movers

8 What helps diggers grab lots of earth at once?

Answer: Teeth

Trains

1 How does the driver see in the dark?

A: With headlamps

2 What 'G' do freight trains carry?

A: Goods

3 How many wagons did the longest freight train have?

Answer: 660

4 Do all trains have just one engine?

Answer: No. The longest-ever train had 16.

5 All trains are powered by diesel. True or false?

Answer: False. They are also powered by electricity.

6 What comes from overhead wires?

Answer: Electric power

7 Unjumble TNSOIAT to name where people get on and off.

Answer: STATION

8 How fast are the quickest trains?

Answer: The fastest trains can go 574 kilometres per hour.

Ships

1 What 'W' do warships have?

Answer: Weapons

2 What are warships usually part of?

Answer: A navy

3 Which kind of ship carries goods?

Answer: Cargo ships

4 Unjumble TONSERNAIC, which cranes lift onto the deck.

Answer: CONTAINERS

5 Some tankers carry oil. True or false?

Answer: True

6 Where are ships controlled from?

Answer: The bridge

7 Where would you sleep on a liner?

Answer: In a cabin

8 How many passengers can the biggest cruise ship carry?

Answer: 4,300

Aeroplanes

1 What does a jet engine suck in at the front?

Answer: Air

2 What helps lift the plane into the air?

Answer: Flaps on the wings

3 Aeroplanes cruise at what speed?

Answer: 700 to 900 kilometres per hour

4 Unjumble YURWAN, where planes take off.

Answer: RUNWAY

5 Who makes sure the planes land safely?

Answer: Air-traffic controllers

6 Who re-fuels the planes?

Answer: Airport ground crew

7 There are different sections for people and what?

Answer: Luggage

8 How many passengers can big planes carry?

Answer: More than 500

Rockets

1 Are some parts meant to fall off?

Answer: Yes

2 Change LOLOPA into the craft that went to the moon.

Answer: APOLLO

3 Are space shuttles re-usable?

Answer: Yes

4 How many astronauts does the orbiter carry?

Answer: As many as seven

5 What is attached to the fuel tank for extra power?

Answer: Booster rockets

6 Does the whole of the space shuttle go into space?

Answer: No. Only the orbiter does.

7 The fuel tank holds only 2 litres of fuel. True or false?

Answer: False. It holds 2 million litres of fuel.

8 What 'P' bring the boosters back?

Answer: Parachutes

Index

A

aerodynamics 115
aeroplanes 124–125, 126
Africa 35, 44, 45, 79
afterlife 106, 107
air-traffic controllers 125
albatrosses 74–75
Albertosaurus 11
Allosaurus 10
Amazon species 43
animals, farm 52–53
animals, jungle 42–43
animals, land 25–58
Antarctica 72
ants 48–49
Apatosaurus 14
apes 44–45
Archelon 18
Arctic Ocean 67
Argentina 81
Asia 30, 34, 36, 44
Australia 22, 35

B

baleen plates 61
bamboo 38, 39
beaches 96–97
bears 36–37, 38–39
bees 36, 37
beetles 46–47
birds 20, 43, 81
    flightless birds 34–35
    wading birds 70–71
birth, giving 22, 31, 41, 57, 61
Brachiosaurus 16–17
breathing 46, 60, 63
breeds, animal 53, 55, 57
Brontosaurus 14
Bronze Age 102–103
bugs 46–47
butterflies and moths 50–51

C

calves, whale 61
camouflage 30, 66, 78
cars 112–113, 114–115, 126

cassowaries 34
cats and breeds 56–57
cattle and breeds 53, 80
chicks and chickens 52, 72, 74
cities 92–93
claws 9, 11, 13, 31, 36, 47
Coelophysis 9
coffins (ancient Egypt) 107
colouring 30, 38, 40, 45, 51,
    78
crocodiles, ancient 9
cubs 29, 31, 33, 39, 41

D

deforestation 83
Deinonychus 11
detection system, electricity 69
diggers 118–119, 126
Dimorphodon 20, 21
dinosaurs 7–24
diving 73, 109
dogs and breeds 54–55
dolphins 19, 62–63

E

earth movers 119
earthquakes 87, 88–89
eggs 9, 23, 48, 49, 51, 52,
    70, 72, 74
Egypt, ancient 104–105, 106
elephants 10, 26–27, 82
embalming 106
emus 35
eyes 38, 65, 69

F

farming 52–53, 80, 94–95,
    105
fighting 15, 29, 47
fins 63, 65, 68
fish 21, 37, 47, 63, 64, 67, 69,
    70, 71, 73
flippers 60, 63, 66
floods 87, 90
flukes, tail 60, 65
flying 20–21, 75

forests 32, 34, 36, 38, 39, 78,
    82, 85
fur 30, 38, 40, 57, 66

G

gauchos 81
glaciers 85
gliding 75
Globidens 19
gods (ancient Egypt) 104
gorillas 44
grasslands 28, 78, 79, 80–81

H

hairy coats 23, 28, 57
Hannibal 26, 27
harvesting 95, 105
home, life at 98–99
Hummers 113
hunting for prey 10, 12, 13,
    23, 28, 29, 30, 31, 32,
    37, 40, 41, 43, 56, 63,
    64, 67, 68, 69, 71, 72, 73
hydraulics 117

I

ice 40, 41, 66, 67, 73
ichthyosaurs 19
insects 21, 47, 50, 51, 70
irrigation 105

J

Japan 89, 92
jaws 9, 16, 21, 49, 54
jewels 107
jungles 30, 42, 43, 82–83

K

kittens 57
krill 61

L

ladybirds 46, 47
largest species 10, 14, 17, 21,
    26, 34, 35, 36, 40, 47,
    58, 60, 74, 76

larvae 48, 49
leaping 63
legs 9, 11, 13, 16, 34, 47
lions 28–29, 56
lizards, ancient 9
logging 82

M

magma 87
mammals, early 22–23
mandrills 45
marsupials 22
meat-eaters 9, 10–11, 12, 13,
    28, 29, 30, 31, 32, 33,
    36, 54, 81
megacities 92
milk 27, 41, 52, 53, 80
Minis (cars) 112
monkeys 44–45
   howler monkeys 43, 45
Morocco 91
Mount Everest 84, 110
mountains 27, 39, 84–85, 91
mummies 106–107

N

Nile river 104, 105
nomads, Maasai 79
North America 10, 11, 13, 36
North Pole 40
nothosaurs 19

O

ocean life 18, 19, 64, 67
orbiters 127
orcas (killer whales) 64
ostriches 35

P

packs, wolf 32, 33
pampas 81
pandas 38–39
penguins 72–73
people and places 77–110
pets 54, 55, 56, 57
pharaohs 105, 107

pigs and piglets 53
pirates 108, 109
Placodus 18, 19
plant-eaters 9, 11, 14–15, 16,
    17, 27, 35, 38, 39, 81
plesiosaurs 19
ploughing 95
polar bears 40–41
prey 10, 11, 13, 21, 23, 36
prides (of lions) 29
Pteranodon 20
pterosaurs 9, 20, 21
puppies 55

R

racing cars 114–115
rainforests 42, 43, 78
record breakers 24, 58, 76,
    110, 128
reptiles, ancient sea 18–19
reptiles, flying 20–21
rhino, Javan 43
rockets 126–127
rockpools 96
running 9, 11, 13, 21, 33,
    34, 35

S

sauropods 9
savannah 28, 78–79
school, at 100–101
   assessments 101
   curriculum 101
   equipment 100
scooping 75
sea creatures 18, 59–76
seabirds 64, 97
seals 19, 41, 64, 66–67
sharks 68–69
sheep 53, 80
shellfish 18, 19, 67, 73
ships 122–123
skin 43, 46, 52
skyscrapers 93
smell, sense of 12, 17, 54
sounds, making 17, 33, 45
South America 43

South Pole 72
spacecraft 126, 127
speed records 126
spyhopping 65
squid 69, 73, 75
Stegosaurus 15
survival 23, 78
swimming 47, 66, 68, 73

T

tails 43, 44, 49, 60
teeth 9, 10, 12, 13, 16, 17,
    19, 54, 68
theropods 9
tigers 30–31, 56
Tokyo 89, 92
tools 102, 103
trains 120–121
treasure, buried 108–109
trees 16, 27, 31, 36, 80, 85
tribes 83
Triceratops 15
trucks 116–117, 126
tusks 26, 27
Tyrannosaurus rex 12–13, 23

U

USA 92, 93

V

villages 90–91
volcanoes 86–87

W

warships 122
weapons 102, 103
whales, blue 14, 60–61
whales, killer 64–65
wings 20, 21, 34, 47, 51, 73,
    74, 75
wolves 11, 32–33, 54

Z

zebras 28, 78

Acknowledgements

The publisher would like to thank the following for permission to reproduce their photographs. Every care has been taken to trace copyright holders. However, it there have been unintentional omissions or failure to trace copyright holders, we apologize and will, if informed, endeavour to make corrections in any future edition.

Page 12 Corbis/Louie Psihoyos; 35 Shutterstock/Cre8tive Images; 39 Corbis/Keren Su; 41 Ardea/M. Watson; 47 Shutterstock/Tomasz Pietryszek; 54 Shutterstock/iofoto; 62–63 Alamy/Steve Bloom Images; 75 Alamy/ImageState; 79 Alamy/Bill Bachmann; 81 Alamy/David W. Hamilton; 82 Alamy/Dbimages; 83 Alamy/Deco Images; 84–85 Shutterstock/Andrew Buckin; 92 Corbis/José Fuste Raga/zefa; 93 Shutterstock/Mario Savoia; 96 Alamy/Bubbles Photolibrary; 99 (top) Alamy/ Stock Connection Distribution; 99 (bottom) Shutterstock/Terrie L. Zeller; 100 Getty/Stone; 101 Shutterstock/Photocreate; 109 Alamy/Paul Ives; 112 Alvey & Towers; 113 Corbis/Dick Reed.